DURCH STARTEN ENGLISCH

8

ÜBUNGSBUCH

Verfasser: Franz Zach und René Gromes

Diesem Buch ist ein Lösungsheft zu den Übungen beigelegt.

Entspricht der Rechtschreibreform 2006

Bibliografische Information der Deutschen Bibliothek:
Die Deutsche Bibliothek verzeichnet diese Publikation in der Deutschen Nationalbibliografie; detaillierte bibliografische Daten sind im Internet über http://dnb.ddb.de abrufbar.

VERITAS-VERLAG, Linz
www.durchstarten.at

Lektorat: Klaus Kopinitsch
Grafische Gestaltung: Ingrid Zuckerstätter
Illustrationen: Helmut »Dino« Breneis
Satz: satz@wolkerstorfer.at
Herstellung: Julia Dresch

Gedruckt in Österreich auf umweltfreundlich hergestelltem Papier

8. Auflage 2019 ISBN 978-3-7058-6845-8

VERITAS
Gemeinsam besser lernen

INHALT – von A bis Z

Hello everybody!

Herzlichen Glückwunsch zum Kauf von **"DURCHSTARTEN – DEIN ÜBUNGSBUCH!"** Du hast damit über 2.000-mal die Gelegenheit, wichtige Punkte der englischen **Grammatik** zu wiederholen und zu üben und gleichzeitig auch deine **Vokabelkenntnisse und deinen Stil** zu verbessern. Das wird dir mehr Sicherheit und Selbstvertrauen im Umgang mit der englischen Sprache verleihen!

Jeder Abschnitt des Buches beginnt mit einer (wirklich) **kurzen Darstellung der Regeln und Ausnahmen**, und dann kommen **Übungen, Übungen** und nochmals **Übungen.**
Selbstverständlich gibt es auch ein **Lösungsheft**, damit du siehst, wie gut du gearbeitet hast.
Vokabelverzeichnisse am Ende des Buches bieten dir Rat und Hilfe, falls dir einmal die Bedeutung eines Wortes nicht gleich einfällt ...
Außerdem findest du noch eine **Tabelle** mit wichtigen ***"irregular verbs"***.

Zum Abschluss noch ein **Tipp:** Arbeite mit Bleistift! Dann kannst du deine falschen Antworten ausradieren und die Übung später wiederholen!

You can do it!

Viel Erfolg bei der Arbeit
mit dem Buch wünschen dir

Franz und René

ARTICLE – Artikel

(A) DEFINITE ARTICLE – BESTIMMTER ARTIKEL

- Der bestimmte Artikel heißt auf Englisch **immer *"the"***, und zwar unabhängig von Person, Zahl und Geschlecht des Bezugswortes.
- Er wird normalerweise dann verwendet, **wenn bestimmte Personen oder Dinge** gemeint sind.
- Es gibt Fälle, wo man den bestimmten Artikel **verwenden muss**,
- und solche, wo man ihn **nicht verwenden darf**.
- Vor Konsonanten (Mitlauten) wird der bestimmte Artikel **[ðə]** gesprochen,
vor Vokalen (Selbstlauten) aber **[ði:]**.

1 Translate the following sentences into English.

Übersetze die folgenden Sätze ins Englische. Lasse dabei die Beistriche weg.

1. Ich möchte das rote Fahrrad, nicht das weiße.
2. Die Pizza gestern Abend war sehr groß.
3. Der Film über Tornados war sehr spannend.
4. Wer kennt das Mädchen mit den roten Haaren?
5. Jeden Abend geht der alte Mann mit seinem Hund spazieren.
6. Joe besucht die Schule gegenüber vom Park.
7. Das Mädchen dort drüben ist meine Freundin Nadine.
8. Niemand erkannte den Mann auf dem Foto.
9. Der Tower von London war früher ein Gefängnis.
10. Das weiße Pferd auf der Wiese hinter dem Haus gehört unseren Nachbarn.
11. Die Tage vor der Prüfung waren nicht sehr leicht.
12. Der Hamster in Freds Zimmer macht sehr viel Lärm.
13. Mein Vater geht manchmal in das Pub am Ende der Straße.
14. Viele Leute denken noch immer an den Sommer von 1968.
15. Das (!) waren die besten Tage meines Lebens.
16. Wer ist der Mann auf dem Foto? – Ein französischer Ingenieur. Er plante den Suezkanal.
17. Mutter kaufte sich den Bikini mit den roten Streifen.
18. Harry Potter ist der junge Held mit der Narbe auf der (!) Stirn.
19. Die "Titanic" versank im Jahre 1912.
20. Ich möchte den selben Haarschnitt haben wie die Frau auf dem Foto.
21. Bitte gib die Orangen in den Obstkorb und die Milch in den Kühlschrank.
22. Möchtest du den weißen oder den schwarzen Pullover ?
23. Der Winter 2006 war lang und kalt.
24. Die Elefanten aus dem Nationalpark dürfen nicht gejagt werden.
25. Das Gebäude auf der anderen Seite des Flusses ist die alte Universität.
26. Lewis Hamilton ist der Fahrer in dem silbernen Auto.
27. Das neue Snowboard gehört mir, nicht dir.

Der bestimmte Artikel ist erforderlich ...

- **zum Hervorheben** einzelner Menschen, Dinge ... aus einer Gruppe:
  Boys *like playing with cars.* ≠ ***The boys over there*** *are playing with cars.*

- **bei Flüssen, Meeren und Gebirgen:**
  The Mackenzie *is Canada's longest river.*
  I would like to go down ***the Amazon*** *in a little boat.*
  Madagascar is an island in ***the Indian Ocean****.*
  The mountains in the west of North America are called ***the Rockies****.*

- **bei Eigennamen im Plural (Mehrzahl):** Personen, Länder, Inselgruppen ...
  Austria was ruled by ***the Habsburgs*** *for many centuries.*
  It is a 35-hour flight to ***the Cook Islands*** *near Australia.*

- In Verbindung **mit einem Adjektiv** zur Bezeichnung einer Gruppe:
  The rich *should do more to help* ***the poor****.* (Die Reichen ... den Armen ...)
  Many people believe that ***the Germans*** *have no sense of humour.* (... die Deutschen ...)

- In Verbindung **mit einem Superlativ:**
  Joe is ***the best*** *singer in the band.*
  This is ***the most wonderful*** *present that I've ever got!*

In bestimmten Fällen darf kein bestimmter Artikel verwendet werden:

- Bei **Namen von Personen** (in der Einzahl):
  Isabel *and* ***Carlos*** *are from Spain.*
  In the summer holidays we stayed with ***Uncle Jesse*** *and* ***Aunt Lydia****.*
  President Trump *comes from New York.*

- Bei **Namen von Ländern** (Einzahl), **Bergen, Seen, Straßen** und **Plätzen**:
  Our next holiday destination is ***Australia****.*
  Peter lives in ***Tokyo****, the capital of* ***Japan****.*
  Mt. Everest *was first climbed in 1953.*
  The White House is on ***Pennsylvania Avenue****.*

  ▶ **Aber: bestimmter Artikel bei diesen "Ausnahmen":**
  Kevin comes from the United Kingdom, not from the United States.
  Many international tourists come skiing to the Tyrol.
  I think the Matterhorn is the most beautiful mountain on earth.

- **Bei Namen von Zeiteinheiten (Tage, Monate, Jahreszeiten):**
  Today is ***Wednesday****, the ninth of* ***March****.*
  The shortest month of the year is ***February****.*
  I like ***summer*** *better than* ***winter****, but* ***spring*** *is my favourite.*
  I hate ***autumn****, because that's when school starts again.*

  ▶ **Aber: bestimmter Artikel bei bestimmten Zeitangaben:**
  School usually starts on the first Monday in September.
  The summer of 2016 was the hottest ever.

2 Fill in: definite article or no article?

Setze ein: bestimmter Artikel oder kein Artikel?

1. In .... winter .... nights are colder and longer than in .... summer.
2. Dave bought his new snowboard with .... money he got for Christmas.
3. Yesterday .... boys in my class had to go and report to .... headmistress because they had broken .... mirror of .... overhead projector while they were fooling around.
4. Henry was sorry for being late again. He promised to take .... earlier train tomorrow.
5. Dad met Mum for .... first time in .... summer of 1968. It was .... love at .... first sight. Mum says Dad has been .... love of her life, and Dad says .... same about Mum.
6. .... love and .... friendship can prevent a lot of trouble.
7. Loch Ness is in .... north of Scotland. It is .... most famous lake of Scotland.
8. Mum, where's .... salt? – On .... table in front of you! Can't you see it?
9. In .... morning it is usually cooler than during .... day.
10. Most plants need .... water and .... sunlight to grow.
11. .... water in our swimming pool is not yet warm enough for swimming.
12. Where did you buy .... cheese we had after .... dinner last night? – In .... cheese shop next to .... train station. Why? – It was .... best cheese I've ever had.
13. .... coffee comes mostly from South America, but .... coffee you're drinking right now is from Africa. How is it? – It's alright, but .... one you usually serve tastes better.
14. There was a hard rain falling from .... sky when they left .... city.
15. .... fish live in .... sea and .... birds fly through .... air.
16. When I woke up this morning, ... sun was shining through .... windows of my room and .... birds were singing in .... trees outside.
17. I love .... music very much, especially .... music of Beethoven and Brahms.
18. My grandparents worked hard all their life. They didn't have .... time and .... money to go on holidays to .... mountains or to .... sea.
19. .... surfing is a very popular sport among .... young in Hawaii and Australia.
20. I like .... tricks that Harry Potter performs because I like .... magic.
21. .... shirt you are wearing is very dirty. Why didn't you take .... T-shirt I put on .... bed for you?
22. He has a little flat in .... new building next to .... post office in .... Oxford Street.
23. .... life can be very unfair sometimes, don't you think?
24. A biography is a book about .... life of a person.
25. I love .... tea, but .... tea that you serve is very strong sometimes.

26. .... cats often try to catch and eat .... young birds.
27. Look, ... cat has caught a mouse again! This is .... third mouse this week.
28. .... breakfast is served from 7.30 to 10 o'clock in .... morning, and .... dinner from 6.30 to 8.30 in .... evening.
29. .... weather report said there may be .... rain and .... snow in .... afternoon.
30. I liked .... skiing in Switzerland, but .... snow in Austria is better and .... lift tickets are much cheaper here.
31. .... coffee and .... ice cream go very well together. I often put .... whipped cream on both.
32. .... Wilsons live in a house in .... country.
33. In .... past, many people thought .... sun and .... moon were gods.
34. In .... morning, Dad usually takes .... bus to .... work, but he will have to drive when he begins his new job .... next month.
35. My daughter Pascal was born on .... evening of June 6th.
36. After .... lunch, Grandpa often takes a nap on .... couch in .... living room.
37. .... little girl in .... last row of .... bus feels sick. Please tell .... driver to stop.
38. Dad wants to sell .... bike he bought two years ago and get .... new model.
39. In .... summer, we often go hiking in .... Alps.
40. There is a school for .... blind in .... Washington Street.
41. .... Maldives in .... Indian Ocean are very famous for their coral reefs.
42. From 1465 to 1603, England was ruled by .... Tudors. They were followed by .... Stuarts.
43. Some people say .... Nile is .... world's longest river. It rises in .... highlands of Ethiopia and empties into .... Mediterranean Sea with a huge delta.
44. For a long time, ... European settlers in North America were not allowed to cross .... Appalachians.
45. Which is bigger, ... Atlantic Ocean or .... Pacific? – .... Pacific, of course.
46. .... Belgium and .... Netherlands are among the founding members of European Union.
47. Many mountains in .... Himalayas are higher than 8,000 metres.
48. .... Hudson River is named after Henry Hudson, an Englishman who sailed for .... Dutch.
49. In most films, ... good win over .... bad.
50. Last winter, ... Austrian ski team won more competitions than any other team.
51. .... Austrian skiers are among .... best in .... world.
52. Our new neighbours, ... Hendersons, seem to be very nice people.
53. Great Britain is .... largest of .... British Isles.
54. I have .... same maths teacher as my dad had when he went to .... school.

3 Fill in: definite article or no article?

Setze ein: bestimmter Artikel oder kein Artikel?

1. My grandma often told me .... stories before I went to .... bed. I liked .... story of Cinderella and .... Prince best.
2. .... love is like a butterfly – it's beautiful but it does not live long.
3. .... girls in my class all like .... animal films.
4. Look, this is .... new English teacher. I hope he's not as strict as .... old one.
5. .... Australian sheep produce very good wool. – Yes, ... wool that comes from Australia is .... best!
6. Hurry up, boys! .... breakfast is on .... table! If you don't hurry, ... tea will get cold.
7. Did you give .... cat .... milk from .... fridge without warming it?
8. I love .... roses! I often look at .... roses in .... park. I especially like .... smell.
9. .... steel is made of .... iron and other metals, like .... chromium or .... nickel.
10. All my friends are interested in .... history of .... Scottish clans.
11. We must do everything to protect .... nature from .... pollution.
12. .... pollution of .... air is getting more and more serious.
13. It is in .... nature of a dog to chase after .... cats.
14. .... Andes are in .... South America, not in .... Africa.
15. .... America of .... "Wild West" does not exist any more.
16. Luke was born on .... Monday, ... eighth of .... August.
17. Americans celebrate .... "Thanksgiving Day" on .... last Thursday in .... November.
18. Many people call .... New York City .... "Big Apple".
19. I don't like .... summer because it's too hot for me.
20. Enzo's favourite subject at .... school is .... maths, but he doesn't like .... teacher.
21. Without .... car, ... life would be much more complicated today.
22. Who are .... people over there? Do you know them?
23. Dad loves .... cinema. He likes .... films from .... fifties and sixties best.
24. Mum, where's .... apple juice? – In .... cellar, I think.
25. Have you heard .... latest news, Mary? .... Queen of England is going to visit our country.
26. Which is heavier, ... oil or .... water? – .... water, of course.
27. Can I drink .... water from .... well in your garden? – Yes. It tastes excellent.
28. .... nature teaches us that .... life is full of .... dangers.
29. Aunt Maggie writes .... books. All .... books on this shelf were written by her.
30. Do you like .... music, Jessica? – I love it, especially .... music from Latin America.

- **Vorsicht** bei diesen Wörtern:

school	▶	*My dad says he always liked school.* (= das Lernen, den Unterricht) *He went to the school on Main Street.* (= das Gebäude, der Ort)
university	▶	*My sister is at university.* (= Sie studiert dort.) *The university in my hometown is very old.* (= die Einrichtung)
church	▶	*Church was over at 11 o'clock.* (= der Gottesdienst) *Mum's office is opposite the church.* (= das Gebäude, der Ort)
hospital	▶	*I had to stay in hospital for a week.* (= zur Behandlung) *There's a nice park around the hospital.* (= das Gebäude, der Ort)
prison	▶	*They sent him to prison for robbing the bank.* (= als Häftling) *They are tearing down the prison.* (= das Gebäude)
bed	▶	*Where's Emma? – In bed.* (= Sie liegt/schläft noch.) *The bed in my room is from IKEA.* (= der Gegenstand, das Möbel)

4 Fill in: definite article or no article?

Setze ein: bestimmter Artikel oder kein Artikel?

1. What do you need for .... school, Fred? – A compass and a drawing board. .... compass must be made of .... metal, but .... drawing board can be plastic.
2. After his accident, Tom was in .... hospital for .... rest of .... year.
3. How do I get from here to .... hospital, please? – You can take a taxi or .... number 3 bus.
4. I'm tired. I think I'll go to .... bed now. Please don't wake me up too early in .... morning.
5. My brother doesn't like .... job he has got now because he doesn't like .... people there.
6. Mr. Jackson is a good teacher. He really likes .... children.
7. .... children in Mr. Jackson's class all like .... school because their teacher is very nice.
8. When my neighbour was young, he was in .... prison after a car accident.
9. Lots of people have found work in .... new factory in .... nearby town.
10. Guide in Schönbrunn Castle: "Ladies and gentlemen, this is .... bed in which Napoleon slept when he was in Vienna."
11. Hannibal, ... King of Carthage, crossed .... Alps with an army of elephants.
12. My grandparents go to .... church every Sunday morning. .... church is not far from their house, so they can walk there. They need not take .... bus.
13. All my friends are interested in .... sport. .... sport they like best is football, of course.
14. .... people say .... rich get richer, ... poor get poorer.
15. The doctor: "As long as .... fever doesn't go away, you'll have to stay in .... bed."
16. .... Mississippi is .... longest river in .... USA.
17. .... night was so cloudy that we could not see .... moon and .... stars.
18. After .... secondary school I want to go to .... university and study .... medicine.
19. Johnny Cash, ... famous country singer, was in .... prison for taking drugs.

(B) INDEFINITE ARTICLE – UNBESTIMMTER ARTIKEL

- Der unbestimmte Artikel heißt auf Englisch **entweder *"a"*** (vor Vokalen) **oder *"an"*** (vor Konsonanten). Dabei ist nicht die Schreibung, sondern die Aussprache von Bedeutung.
  a ball, a mountain, a stamp **... aber auch** *a uniform* (weil [junifɔm])
  an antelope, an eagle, an iceberg, an upload **... aber auch** *an hour* ([ən auə])

5 Fill in: "a" or "an".

Setze ein: "a" oder "an".

1. Let's go for .... ice cream now!
2. .... old English saying goes like this, ".......... apple .... day keeps the doctor away."
3. People say that .... elephant never forgets .... face.
4. My cousin Tom drives .... Aston Martin. That's .... British car.
5. .... digeridoo is .... typically Australian instrument.
6. .... gun is .... very dangerous thing.
7. My dad is .... early riser. He gets up at 5 o'clock in the morning, even on .... Sunday.
8. My parents had booked .... apartment in .... nice hotel near .... lake.
9. I think I've just had .... excellent idea!
10. Where have you been? We've been waiting for you for over .... hour!
11. Did you see any animals in the mountains? – Oh yes! We saw .... bear and .... eagle.
12. What .... ugly school uniform! Green trousers and .... orange sweater!
13. That's Mr. Bell. He is .... old friend of the family. We've known him for .... very long time.
14. Everybody needs .... good friend or two.
15. .... hour of happiness is more than .... ton of money.
16. Donkeys are quite strong. .... donkey can easily break .... door.
17. .... cow is usually peaceful, but .... bull is often wild.
18. .... jeweller's shop can be .... expensive place for .... man.
19. In every child's room there should be .... bed, ... desk and, of course, ... computer.
20. Kurt is .... honest boy, and that's why everybody likes him.
21. .... penguin is .... bird, but .... whale is not .... fish.
22. .... ant is .... insect, but .... scorpion is not.
23. .... open door or window is .... invitation for .... burglar.
24. We all know that .... lemon tastes sour, but .... apple can be sour, too.
25. Albert Einstein was not .... ordinary man; he was .... genius!
26. My brother has found .... interesting job with .... international company.

▶ **Der unbestimmte Artikel ist erforderlich ...**

- **bei bestimmten Wörtern an "nachgeordneter Stelle"** *(*selten):*

half a(n) ...	▶	*half a litre, half an hour, half a year ...*
What a(n) ...!	▶	*What an idea! What a nice man! What a friendly face! ...*
such a(n) ...	▶	*such a clever girl, such an unusual name, such a sad story ...*
quite a(n) ...	▶	*quite an old car, quite an expensive holiday, quite a nice hotel ...*
so ... a(n) ...*	▶	*so clever a girl, so unusual a name, so sad a story ...*
too ... a(n) ...*	▶	*too crazy an idea, too serious a mistake, too bad an accident ...*

6 Change the following sentences.

Wandle die folgenden Sätze so um, dass der unbestimmte Artikel an "nachgeordneter Stelle" erscheint. Beachte dabei den Lösungsvorschlag.

1. Alice had a clever idea. (What a ...!)
2. The play was so good that I want to see it again. (It was such ...)
3. That was a sad story. Everyone had tears in their eyes. (It was so ... that ...)
4. The film was brilliant. (What ...!)
5. This development is too dangerous. (That's too ...)
6. Her voice was so good that she always sang the leading parts. (She had such ...)
7. The car crash was so bad that the passengers were taken to hospital. (It was so bad ...)
8. The night was too cold for camping. (It was too cold ...)
9. That was a very stupid answer. (What ...!)
10. The question was rather difficult to answer. (That was quite ...)
11. This hotel was too expensive for me. (This was too ...)
12. That's a very old bottle of red wine. (That's quite ...)
13. I'll meet you in 30 minutes in front of the school. (... in half ...)
14. Joe came back from Australia six months ago. (... half ... ago)
15. The film had a very surprising end. (What a ...!)
16. For this cake you need 500 g of flour. (... kilo of flour)
17. The bank robbers got away with 500,000 $. (with ... million dollars)
18. The flight to Australia was quite long. (It was quite ...)
19. 1955 was an important year for Austria. We will never forget it. (... such ... that ...)
20. The wind was so strong that we could not go sailing. (There was too ... for sailing.)
21. The party was so nice that nobody wanted to go home. (It was such ...)
22. The last foreign soldiers left our country 50 years ago. (... century ago.)
23. Let's meet in thirty minutes. (... half ...)
24. This film is too horrible for young children. (This is too ...)
25. Christine is quite good at skiing. (She is quite a ...)
26. Nina is six months older than her boyfriend. (... half ...)
27. This is a wonderful surprise! Jackie is coming tomorrow! (What ...!)
28. The hotel was so expensive that we did not stay. (It was such ...)
29. Lisa was quite shocked when she heard the news. (It was quite ... for Lisa when ...)
30. This is an excellent plan, Joe! (What ...!)

▶ **Der Artikel ist weiters erforderlich bei ...**

- **bestimmten Angaben über eine Person:**

Beruf	▶	*My older sister wants to be* ***a lawyer****.* *Joe's father is* ***an engineer****.*
Herkunft	▶	*In my summer holidays I met* ***an American*** *from San Francisco.* *Many jokes begin like this, "****An Austrian*** *and* ***a German*** *were talking ..."*
Religion	▶	*The Pope is* ***a Catholic*** *and the Dalai Lama is* ***a Buddhist****.*

▶ **Kein Artikel bei ...**

- **Titel, die es nur einmal gibt:**

Bill Clinton was ***President*** *for eight years.*
My brother was ***captain*** *of the football team from 2003 to 2005.*
Prince William will be ***King of England*** *one day.*

- **unzählbaren Dingen:**

Milk *and* ***orange juice*** *have lots of vitamins.*
Many people cannot find ***work*** *these days.*
I need ***money*** *to buy* ***food****.*

7 Fill in: "a" or "an" or nothing.

Setze ein: "a" oder "an" oder nichts.

1. .... sheep eats .... grass.
2. You eat .... soup with .... spoon.
3. They made me .... leader of their gang.
4. Susan was elected .... captain of the basketball team.
5. In the mountains we drank .... water from .... well.
6. Cows give us .... milk, and we make .... butter and .... cheese from it.
7. You need .... glass to make .... window like this.
8. .... grass always grows best where there is .... water and .... sunlight.
9. Every Saturday .... boat arrives with .... group of tourists.
10. .... cat likes to eat .... meat and to drink .... milk.
11. Sandra's mum works as .... nurse in .... hospital.
12. .... fish needs .... water to survive.
13. Today, ... car has .... radio.
14. They had to live on .... bread and .... water for some days.
15. Most people cut .... steak with .... knife.
16. .... novel is a piece of .... literature.

17. We all need .... air to breathe.

18. Without .... light there would be .... darkness.

19. .... tea is usually served hot.

20. .... hungry person must have .... food.

21. In winter there is sometimes .... ice on the windows.

22. There is still .... dirt on your trousers.

23. Elizabeth II was crowned .... queen when she was 27 years old.

24. .... poetry is sometimes boring for .... student.

25. There is often .... sand on .... Italian beach.

26. I like .... butter and .... jam on .... slice of bread.

27. Mrs. Greene has been .... headmistress of our school for half .... year.

28. What does your dad do, Tommy? – He's .... bus driver. He drives .... school bus.

29. Many people like .... cheese with .... wine.

30. We could see .... smoke over .... house in .... town.

31. Aunt Nelly was made .... president of her women's club.

32. My grandmother was .... housewife for over 50 years.

33. Cutlery is made of .... metal or .... wood.

34. I eat .... apple every morning before I go to .... school.

35. After .... long debate Charlie was elected .... head boy of his school.

36. My brother likes .... meat for dinner, but I prefer .... fish or .... vegetables.

37. Can I have .... breakfast now? I'd like .... toast with jam and .... cup of tea, please.

38. I think my sister wants to be .... lawyer when she grows up.

39. Yoghinder and Rajiv are from India. Yoghinder is .... Sikh and Rajiv is .... Hindu.

40. Ali doesn't eat .... ham because he is .... Muslim.

41. Every year, the last school day is .... Friday.

42. Linda's mum is .... dentist. She has .... office in .... building in the town centre.

43. What .... wonderful idea! .... pizza with .... ham and .... cheese!

44. .... "ulu" is .... kind of knife that is used by the Inuit in Alaska.

45. In our country, people have .... high standard of living.

46. I think somebody has just climbed into the neighbours' house through .... open window.

47. Your dad is .... policeman. Let's call him!

48. Do you have .... computer? I would like to write .... email.

49. Mr. Maxwell has been .... farmer all his life. He owns quite .... big farm in .... village nearby.

50. For breakfast I usually have .... tea, but sometimes I have .... cup of coffee.

8 Fill in: "a", "an", "the" or nothing.

Setze ein: "a", "an", "the" oder nichts.

1. There is .... ugly insect in my juice. I hate .... juice with insects!
2. .... photos on .... USB stick are of .... woman who walked all the way to .... North Pole and back.
3. It is nice to play .... game of chess in .... café with .... good friend.
4. .... people love .... water and .... sunshine.
5. We liked .... bananas Mum brought home yesterday. They were so sweet.
6. Look, there are .... big black clouds in .... sky. There's going to be .... thunderstorm. I think you'd better take .... umbrella with you.
7. What .... lovely day! .... white clouds over .... lake are so beautiful!
8. My mum is .... teacher at .... school that she attended herself when she was .... child.
9. .... first day of school was .... so exciting day for Steven that he couldn't fall asleep that night.
10. .... life can be hard, but .... life of my dog isn't! .... dog has .... easy life indeed!
11. F. D. Roosevelt was .... President of the United States from 1932 to 1945. He was .... only president who was elected four times.
12. Mum and Dad are fond of .... glass of wine in .... evening, after .... work.
13. .... good pupil always works hard for .... school.
14. You need .... telescope to watch .... stars.
15. .... boat is made of .... wood, ... metal or .... plastic.
16. I like .... cup of tea with .... milk and .... sugar in the morning.
17. My mum likes .... operas very much, especially .... operas by Verdi.
18. .... garden often has .... pretty flowers in it, but .... flowers in your garden are .... most beautiful ones I have ever seen.
19. Mr. Smith has gone to .... conference. You have missed him by half .... minute.
20. It is .... nature of .... lion to hunt and kill.
21. Jan lives in .... Netherlands. He is .... fisherman. He works in .... North Sea.
22. It is very nice to read .... book in .... bed before falling asleep.
23. Look, ... boys in .... park are playing with .... model car!
24. Where did you buy .... bread that we had for .... breakfast this morning? – At .... new shop opposite .... train station. They get it from .... baker who has won many prizes for his bread.
25. What .... strange story! Who told you? – I heard it from Frank half .... hour ago.
26. This is Mr. Brown. He is .... Chief of Police in .... town where I live. It's .... hard job.

CONJUNCTIONS – Bindewörter

Eine Liste der wichtigsten Bindewörter:

although (though)	obwohl		**aber**	*but, however*
and	und		**als**	*when, as*
as	da, als		**außerdem**	*besides*
as well as	und, sowie, wie auch		**da**	*as*
because	weil		**daher**	*so, ...*
besides	außerdem		**damit**	*so that*
both ... and	sowohl ... als auch		**dann**	*then*
but	aber, sondern		**denn**	*for*
either ... or	entweder ... oder		**deshalb**	*so*
for	denn		**entweder ... oder**	*either ... or*
however	jedoch		**jedoch**	*however*
neither ... nor	weder ... noch		**nicht nur ...**	*not only ...*
not only ...	nicht nur ...		**sondern auch**	*but also*
but also	sondern auch		**obwohl**	*although*
or	oder		**oder**	*or*
so	also, daher		**sodass**	*so that*
(so) that	sodass, damit		**sondern**	*but*
that	der (welcher), die ...		**sowie**	*as well as*
then	dann		**und**	*and, as well as*
when	als		**während**	*while*
which	der, die, das		**weder ... noch**	*neither ... nor*
who	welcher, welche, welches		**weil**	*because*

9 Fill in: and, but, because, so, or, (so) that, who, which, that, when, then.

Setze ein: and, but, because, so, or, (so) that, who, which, that, when, then.

1. Mum was very tired, ... she could not fall asleep. .... she took a pill.
2. .... Dad comes home from work, he lies down on the sofa .... he is tired.
3. Do you have any idea .... will be our Latin teacher next year? I hope it won't be Miss Nolan .... Mr. Smythe!
4. The platypus is one of the strangest animals .... I have ever seen. It lays eggs like a bird .... a reptile, ... it also nurses (*stillen*) its young, like a mammal.
5. Tina Petersen, ... has been my friend since kindergarten, will move to Manchester at the end of the school year .... her dad has found a better job there.
6. South Africa is great! .... we were there last year, we went to Cape Town first. We stayed for a week, and .... we went on to Durban and Johannesburg.
7. Max had a headache yesterday, ... he did not come to basketball practice. His mum gave him an aspirin .... told him to lie down.
8. This is Toby's new mountain bike, ... he got from his parents. He locks it into the garage every evening .... nobody can take it away.
9. Dad plays tennis .... he jogs, ... he doesn't ski any more.

10. Of course I'll help you .... are my best friend.

11. Before I go to bed, I always take a shower .... I brush my teeth.

12. Yesterday I missed the bus, ... I had to walk home from school.

13. George says he will come to the cinema with us, ... he doesn't really want to.

14. We only got seats in the last row .... we didn't really see what was going on.

15. Those of you .... would like to go swimming tomorrow please raise their hands!

16. You must pick up all the rubbish .... is lying on the floor.

17. My friends and I were watching TV .... Mum said we would have to go shopping.

18. Let me take off my shoes first, ... I will tell you the end of the story.

19. We hid the Easter eggs so well .... we could not find them any more.

20. The police interviewed everyone .... had seen the accident.

21. Please call me at 743-5423 .... send me an email.

22. "Awesome!" is the only word .... comes to my mind if we talk about Disney World.

23. The film was absolutely boring, ... we left before it was over.

24. Dad was waiting for the tram .... it started to rain. He got very wet ....
he had forgotten to take an umbrella, ... now he has a cold.

25. First you cut out the pictures, ... you glue them into your album.

26. Are you coming to the cinema with us, Karen, ... are you too tired?

27. Jacob did everything to finish the project in time, ... his friends didn't do their share of the work. .... they handed in their work three days late, ... they all got bad marks.

28. Helen stumbled .... she was running across the street, ... she fell .... hurt her knees.

29. Every evening we could watch the animals .... came out of the jungle to drink.

30. .... everyone was there, we could begin.

31. One of the musicians had the flu, ... the band had to cancel the concert.

32. Four people were hurt in the accident, ... nobody was killed.

33. We wanted to go and see "The Mummy", ... they didn't show it any more.
.... we saw "Dune" instead, ... it was quite good.

34. We shut the windows .... turned off the lights, and .... we went to bed.

35. My grandparents still live in the house .... they built after they got married.

36. The wine .... comes from this region is called "Zierfandler".

37. Everybody is crazy about Martina, ... I think Julia is much nicer .... she never makes fun of other people.

10 Fill in: "although" or "but". *Setze ein: "although" oder "but".*

example: *Although* it was hot, the children played outside. It was hot, *but* the children played outside.

1. Tony wasn't very hungry, ... he ate three hamburgers.
2. .... Carina was very tired, she watched TV until 2 o'clock in the morning.
3. David got only a "C" on his history project, ... his dad had helped him with it.
4. The children ran as fast as they could, ... they missed their train by two minutes.
5. Jenny forgot to return the books, ... her mum had reminded her three times.
6. .... my dad likes jazz, he doesn't often listen to it.
7. I would like to learn Japanese, ... I don't know anybody who could teach me.
8. The tourists decided to climb the mountain .... the weather was not too good.
9. .... Kevin knew who had taken my biro, he did not tell me.
10. Everybody knows Harry, ... nobody wants to give me his phone number.

11 Make sentences, using "although" or "but".

Bilde Sätze mit Hilfe von "although" und "but".

example: Mum, not go to bed – be tired ▶ Mum did not go to bed *although* she was tired.
Mum, be tired – not go to bed ▶ Mum was tired, *but* she did not go to bed.

1. the kids, play computer games – their mum, want to sleep

....

2. Dave, switch on, light in the kitchen – he, not wake up his parents

....

3. the cat, be thirsty – it, not drink the milk

....

4. I, not really like the film – I, watch it three times

....

5. Granny, not see much any more – she, not like wearing glasses

....

6. Mario, be only 17 – he, sometimes drive his dad's car

....

7. Fred, still have a lot of work to do – he, not start yet

....

8. Aunt Dorothy, be allergic to cats – she, keep two cats in her flat

....

9. our old professor, be a real genius – he, always forget his umbrella at school

....

"as" anstelle von ***"because"*** oder ***"when/while"***
(Grund) **(Zeit)**

Grund: *Ron hid behind the curtains because he was afraid.*
As Ron was afraid, he hid behind the curtains.
*Ron hid behind the curtains **as** he was afraid.*

Zeit: *While we were driving through the country, we saw lots of nice villages.*
As we were driving through the country, we saw lots of nice villages.

12 Use "as" instead of "because" or "when/while".

Verwende "as" anstelle von "because" oder "when/while".

1. We did not want to play another game because it was late.
2. Mum did not allow us to go out because it was already 9 o'clock.
3. I will never smoke because it is expensive and bad for my health.
4. While we were driving through Oklahoma, we expected to see a tornado.
5. We noticed a strange smell in the house when we entered the room.
6. When the sun rose, most of the animals disappeared into the jungle.
7. Dad did not want to go to the concert because he had a headache.
8. I was not allowed to eat cake or chocolate because the doctor had forbidden all sweet things.
9. They took away Uncle Edgar's driving licence because they caught him drunk again.
10. We were all surprised that the boy played the piano so well because he is only six years old.
11. They came into the room without knocking because the door was open.
12. While I was talking to Michael, I had a wonderful idea.
13. When the alarm clock started to ring, Sandy slowly opened her eyes.
14. We decided to look for another hotel because the people were extremely unfriendly.
15. When it was getting too dark to see, we decided to stop for the day.
16. Sammy found a bunch of keys while he was walking to the bus stop.
17. We did not try to catch the train because it was too late already.
18. When we were leaving the church, the sun was setting behind the houses.
19. We were soon lost because nobody knew the way.
20. Bill called while I was getting ready to go to bed.
21. The teacher watched the boys while they were smoking cigarettes on the toilet.
22. Brian called a taxi because he could not start his car this morning.
23. Bettina decided to see a doctor because her stomach ache was getting worse.
24. Carla has a wonderful suntan because she spends a lot of time outdoors.
25. Fred started to shake when he heard the news.
26. Jennifer will find a job easily because she is clever and hard working.
27. When no one opened the door, we left again.
28. We asked for directions because we did not know the way.
29. When the dog started barking, the two burglars ran away.
30. The whole family woke up when Sally switched on the lights.
31. Henry was not allowed to leave the country because he had forgotten to bring his passport.
32. When I woke up this morning, it was raining cats and dogs.
33. They did not let us in because we had no tickets.

"as well as" und *"both ... and"* anstelle von *"and"*

The Maxwells are our neighbours and our friends.

The Maxwells are our neighbours ***as well as*** *our friends.*
The Maxwells are ***both*** *our neighbours* ***and*** *our friends.*

13 Use "as well as" and "both ... and" instead of "and".

Verwende "as well as" und "both ... and" anstelle von "and".

1. March 21 and September 23 are called "equinox".
2. Sammy collects minerals and CDs.
3. Jack and Tony like dark-haired girls.
4. The film about sharks was informative and exciting.
5. April and June have thirty days.
6. We have asked Brian and Kevin about the reasons for their fight.
7. The "Star Wars" films are funny and sad.
8. The English King or Queen is still the head of state in Canada and in Australia.
9. My dad speaks English and Spanish.
10. Sandra is intelligent and hard working.
11. Our new car is comfortable and economical.
12. Trumpets and trombones are difficult to play.
13. The children were wet and cold when they came home in the evening.
14. Robert was sad and disappointed when he had finished reading the letter.
15. My grandfather and my grandmother were born in January.
16. Honda makes cars and motorcycles.
17. Liza Minelli is a singer and a dancer.
18. To me, reading is relaxing and exciting.
19. Fish and meat will be served for dinner.
20. Georgia and Armenia are rather small countries.
21. Austria is a member of the United Nations and the European Union.
22. Shakespeare wrote comedies and tragedies.
23. School can be interesting and boring.
24. My parents and my grandparents paid for my new room.
25. I use my PC for work and for play.
26. On Sundays and on holidays the restaurant is closed.
27. Our central heating runs on gas and wood.
28. Frieda's parents are nice and strict.
29. I hope that Harry and Willie will be at the party.
30. Michiko speaks and writes Japanese very well.
31. Dad planned and built our weekend house himself.
32. Flight attendants must be able to speak English and another foreign language.
33. The climate is getting warmer and wetter.
34. The price includes accommodation and meals.

"both … and"	▶	sowohl … als auch	→	*Sue is **both** clever **and** pretty.*
"either … or"	▶	entweder … oder	→	*She is **either** at school **or** at home.*
"neither … nor"	▶	weder … noch	→	*She likes **neither** fruit **nor** vegetables.*

14 Connect the following sentences with "both … and", "either … or" or "neither … nor".

Verbinde die folgenden Sätze mit "both … and", "either … or" oder "neither … nor".

examples:

Sue is clever and she is pretty, too. ▶ *Sue is **both** clever **and** pretty.*
She is at school or she is at home. ▶ *She is **either** at school **or** at home.*
She doesn't like fruit and she doesn't like vegetables. ▶ *She likes **neither** fruit **nor** vegetables.*

1. You can have tea for breakfast. Or you can have coffee. (either … or)
2. The weather was perfect. It was not too cold and not too hot. (neither … nor)
3. Austria's flag is red and white. (both … and)
4. Tom is not very intelligent and he isn't hard working, so he has problems at school. (neither … nor)
5. In the winter holidays we go to Italy or we stay in Austria. (either … or)
6. Spring and summer are my favourite seasons of the year. (both … and)
7. This year we won't make summer holidays and we won't make winter holidays. (neither … nor)
8. Uncle Edward lives and works in Birmingham now. (both … and)
9. Boys must wear suits or jackets and trousers. (either … or)
10. You can help me in the kitchen or in the garden, whatever you like.
11. Claudia spent more than fifteen years in Greece, so she speaks and writes Greek perfectly.
12. My brother hasn't fed the dog and I haven't fed the dog; Mum will be angry.
13. You can listen to music or you can study, but you can't do both.
14. I don't eat meat and I don't eat sausages. I'm a vegetarian, you see.
15. Alcohol and nicotine are illegal for kids under sixteen.
16. The food in Turkey is cheap and excellent.
17. People keep mice or they keep cats, but never both.
18. Luke is a poor student, so he doesn't have a car and he doesn't have a motorbike.
19. No homework again, Mike? You must be stupid or lazy. Which is it?
20. I hope the room has satellite TV and cable TV.
21. We can go to the cinema or we can stay at home. What would you like?
22. My sister and I sing in this year's Christmas concert.
23. Don't ask Maria for help. She isn't nice and she isn't generous.
24. Give me the money tomorrow or I will tell your parents.
25. Mr. Landau is a really nice person. He is helpful and polite towards everybody.
26. We all love gardening. It is good for the body and for the soul.
27. Norman did not get my email, and Frank did not get it. I don't understand this.
28. Tidy up your rooms or we won't go to the pizzeria today. It's up to you.
29. My mum doesn't smoke and my dad doesn't smoke. So, why should I?
30. Before a match, Sebastian is excited and nervous.
31. The Greeks did not build pyramids and the Romans didn't build any, but the Egyptians did.
32. Adrian likes pork and he likes beef, so we should get both for the barbecue.
33. Sylvia leaves for England on Friday or Saturday, I'm not sure.

"both ... and"	▶ sowohl ... als auch	→	*Sue is **both** clever **and** pretty.*
"not only ... but also"	▶ nicht nur ... sondern auch	→	*She is **not only** clever, **but also** pretty.*

15 Replace "and" with "both ... and" and "not only ... but also".

Ersetze "and" durch "both ... and" und "not only ... but also" (siehe Beispiel oben).

1. Learning foreign languages is interesting and important.
2. July and August have thirty-one days.
3. I have talked to Mum and Dad about a new mountain bike.
4. The "Batman" films are fun and exciting.
5. Nigeria and India use English as an official language.
6. Suzy is pretty and clever.
7. Bernie sings and dances like Michael Jackson.
8. Coffee and bananas come from the tropics.
9. Ferraris and Lamborghinis are expensive sports cars.
10. Johann Strauß Father and Johann Strauß Son were excellent composers.
11. Elephants are strong and clever.
12. The book Grandma gave me for my birthday is exciting and well written.
13. Tom is Dave's neighbour in class and his best friend.
14. Sally's new boyfriend is handsome and rich.
15. The lecture was long and boring.
16. Aunt Dorothy won the tennis finals and the women's high jump in her age group.
17. Today, most kids have mobile phones and MP3-players.
18. We did not want to stay any longer because we were tired and very hungry.
19. Dinner at the "Shangri La" was excellent and surprisingly cheap.
20. Grandpa brought presents for us children and for our parents.
21. Lisa and Linda like athletic boys.
22. The documentary about the Second World War was interesting and shocking.
23. I will never smoke because it is expensive and bad for my health.
24. Vienna and Bratislava are on the Danube.
25. Driving fast is stupid and dangerous.
26. Tom Hanks won Oscars for "Philadelphia" and for "Forrest Gump".
27. Petrol and medical drugs can be made from crude oil.
28. Cortina and St. Moritz are world famous winter resorts.
29. Big cities can be exciting and dangerous.
30. The sun and the wind will be used more often to produce energy.
31. This year the month of June was wetter and cooler than last year.
32. After the marathon, the runners were tired and happy.
33. Malawi and Zambia are former British colonies in Africa.
34. Many people in Canada speak English and French.
35. Christmas and Easter are important Christian holidays.
36. Hillary and Bill will come to the conference next month.
37. What you have just said is wrong and stupid.

"however" und *"but"*

"but"	**= aber**	▶	*Charlie is usually late,* ***but*** *today he was on time.*
"however"	**= jedoch**	▶	*Charlie is usually late. Today,* ***however,*** *he was on time.* *Charlie is usually late.* ***However,*** *today he was on time.* *Charlie is usually late. Today he was on time,* ***however.***

16 Replace "but" with "however" and "however" with "but".

Ersetze "but" durch "however" und "however" durch "but".

1. Dave wanted to buy a CD drive, but he did not know where to go.
2. Sally invited me to her party last weekend. However, I had to say no because I had the flu.
3. Columbus wanted to sail to India, but he discovered a new continent.
4. My parents drove to Salzburg to see "Jedermann". When they got there, however, they could not get any tickets.
5. Reinhold Messner has climbed the highest mountains on earth and he has walked across Greenland, but an accident forced him to give up his plan to walk from Siberia to Canada.
6. Everybody always tells me how great the Harry Potter books and films are. I don't really like such stories, however.
7. Sally was at home waiting for Dave, but he had forgotten the date and was watching TV.
8. Dad had made great plans for this year's holidays. However, he had a little accident last Sunday and so we can't go now.
9. We wanted to eat out at "Le Bistro", but when we saw the menu we went to McDonald's instead.
10. Simon usually rides his bike to school. Today, however, it was so cold that he took the bus.

"for" **= denn** ▶ anstelle von *"because"* oder *"as"* (nicht an erster Stelle)

17 Replace "because" and "as" with "for".

Ersetze "because" und "as" durch "for".

1. Everyone expected our team to win the finals because we had the best players.
2. As Jacob was the last to arrive, he missed the beginning of the film. (word order!)
3. You should ask Charlie because he is the expert!
4. As nobody seemed to be hungry, we did not stop for a rest. (word order!)
5. I decided to stay at the "Seven Roses" because it was cheap and the people were friendly.
6. We decided to stop for the day because it was getting too dark to see.
7. As the rain was getting stronger and stronger, they had to cancel the match.
8. As nobody had brought a plan, we did not find the house at once.
9. We could not understand the speaker because the people in front of us were so noisy.
10. As a storm was coming up, the ferryboats could not leave the harbour.
11. Sebastian did not speak to Laura because he had no idea what to say.
12. As we had gone to bed very late last night, we slept until the early afternoon.
13. Alan did not tell his parents because he thought his brother had already done it.
14. The two boys did not talk to each other because they had had a quarrel the day before.

FUTURE – Zukunft

future with "will"

- für zukünftige Ereignisse, über die man keine Kontrolle hat
zB Annahmen, Erwartungen, Hoffnungen, Vorhersagen ...

*My brother thinks he **will get** an iPad next Christmas.*
*Joe likes me. Maybe he **will invite** me to his party.*
*It **will snow** again next winter.*

- für plötzliche Entscheidungen ("ohne viel nachzudenken")

*What? Tomorrow is your birthday? **I'll find** you a nice present!*
*Someone has broken into that car. – We**'ll call** the police.*

- bei Aufforderungen ("höflich, aber bestimmt")

***Will** you **give** me this book, please?*
*Dad, **will** you **tell** Mum that I can't be back before 7 o'clock?*

future with "going to"

- für unmittelbar bevorstehende Handlungen und für feste Pläne oder Absichten (ohne bestimmtes "Datum")

*Take an umbrella with you. It **is going to rain**.*
*I **am going to repair** my bike now.*
*My parents **are going to buy** a bigger car.*

present progressive

- für geplante Vorhaben, für welche die Vorbereitungen laufen oder getroffen sind (fast immer mit "Datum")

*I**'m redecorating** my room <u>at the weekend</u>.*
*Jill **is having a party** <u>on Saturday</u>.*
*We **are leaving** for Italy <u>tomorrow</u>.*

future progressive

- für Handlungen, die zu einem Zeitpunkt in der Zukunft gerade im Verlauf sein werden

*Tomorrow at this time we **will be sitting** on the plane to Toronto.*

- wenn man einer Sache Nachdruck verleihen will, damit sie auch sicher passiert

*If I tell Sam to do it, he **will be doing** it.*

present simple

- nach bestimmten *prepositions of time*:
after, before, when, until, as soon as

*I will call you <u>as soon as</u> I **hear** from Charlie.*
*We'll talk to Joe <u>before</u> he **leaves** the country.*

- bei genauen Zeitangaben (Fahrpläne und dergleichen)

*Grandpa's bus **arrives** <u>at 5.30</u>.*
*The concert **starts** <u>at 8 o'clock</u>.*

18 Future with "will" or with "going to"? Fill in the correct form.

Zukunft mit "will" oder mit "going to"? Setze die richtige Form ein.

1. If Tom is not at home now, I (call) .... him later in the evening.
2. We (visit) .... Aunt Dorothy in hospital soon. – That's nice. I (come) .... with you if you don't mind. Tell me when you go.
3. Sue (be) .... 15 next week. We (have) .... a big celebration for her.
4. Dad is busy right now, but he (play) .... with you as soon as possible.
5. Look, the other team is by far better. We (lose) .... the match again.
6. What you (do) .... after this year, Dave ? – I don't know yet, but I think I (go) .... to a technical school.
7. Somebody is knocking at the door! Who (go) .... let them in?
8. Who are these flowers for, Dave? – I (give) .... them to Betty.
9. If I buy some steaks, (you, cook) .... them for us tonight?
10. Why do you want my notebook? (you, copy) .... my homework?
11. Why have you bought all these brushes? (you, start) .... painting?
12. Mum, (you, wake) .... me up at seven, please?
13. What about that electric drill? (you, break) .... into a bank, my friend?
14. If you hurry, you (be) .... done in five minutes.
15. 400 €? That's too expensive. I (paint) .... the room myself!
16. I (tell) .... the teacher if you don't stop fighting at once!
17. Here's some money, Dave. (you, get) .... me some cigarettes, please?
18. You (be) .... sick if you eat all this ice cream by yourself.
19. (you, wear) .... these shoes to school? You must be crazy!
20. (you, stop) .... that noise now, please? I (not ask) .... you again!
21. (you, leave) .... the car open overnight? I think that's very dangerous.
22. (you, please, be) .... quiet, Sally? I'm trying to read.
23. (you, call) .... him right now or (you, wait) .... for another hour?
24. I've been ill, so they probably (not let) .... me play on Saturday.
25. I'm sorry, I can't stay, but we (meet) .... after school anyway.
26. Mum, the phone is ringing! – Well, I (not answer) .... it.
27. I hope Jim (not talk) .... about me with his friends.

19 Future with "will", "going to", "present simple" or "present progressive"?

Zukunft mit "will", "going to", "present simple" oder "present progressive"?

1. Dave, (you, drive) .... the car into the garage, please?
2. I'm going to the concert now. (you, come) .... with me?
3. I've forgotten to tell the Millers that we can't come today, so I (call) .... them right now if you don't mind.
4. Tom and Harry, (you, please stop) .... that nonsense and sit down? – Sir, we (just, act out) .... the balcony scene from "Romeo and Juliet".
5. Mum, Mr. Black is in hospital. – Well, (you, visit) .... him some time? – I guess so. Maybe we (go) .... tomorrow.
6. What's all this food for, Bob? – Have you forgotten? We (celebrate) .... Betty's birthday tomorrow!
7. What do you need the jack for, Dad? – The car has a puncture, and I (change) .... the wheel.
8. Why are you peeling so many apples, Mum? – I (bake) .... an apple pie, Sally. Perhaps Aunt Susan (stop) .... by in the afternoon.
9. Dave, (you, please shut up) .... ? I'm trying to concentrate!
10. I (attend) .... painting classes next term. I've just registered for them.
11. (you, please switch off) .... the TV and go to bed, Sally?
12. Everybody (be) .... disappointed if you don't tell us about your trip.
13. Are you free this evening? We (play) .... dominoes with Frank and Laura. You can come if you want to.
14. Granny is very nervous. They (operate) .... her knee next week.
15. It's too warm in here. (somebody, open) .... the windows, please?
16. Dad bought a new car for Mum a month ago. It's a surprise, but he is sure she (like) .... it.
17. Our school building is very old, but they (build) .... a new one right beside it next year.
18. Have you heard? Caroline and Nick (get) .... married next month!
19. When I'm older, I (be) .... a millionaire. My family and I (live) .... in a castle and (have) .... lots of cars.
20. The neighbours (go) .... away on holiday tomorrow.
21. (you, go) .... to Paris again next week? – Not next week! Tomorrow! My plane (leave) .... at 8 in the morning.

22. Try this cake, Janet. You (like) .... it.

23. If this headache doesn't go away, I (go) .... crazy.

24. (Grandma,come) .... to visit us again soon? – Yes, next week, I think.

25. (you, fly) .... to London ? – No, I (take) ....

the train. It takes longer, but it's more interesting.

26. We all hope this (never, happen) .... again.

27. These are strange pictures, Doris. I'm afraid nobody (like) .... them.

28. There (be) .... no talking during the test! Do you understand?

29. Jacqueline (sing) .... tonight. They say she's very good.

30. (you, take) .... the dogs to the seaside this summer? – Yes, of course.

31. Mary, what (you, tell) .... the teacher? – I (probably, tell) ....

.... her a lie.

32. When I (have) .... the money, I (pay) ....

you back what I borrowed from you.

33. Laura (leave) .... for Portugal tomorrow morning. She has already

packed her things. – When (her plane, depart) .... ? – Very early, at 7.

34. Bea is nice. We (invite) .... her to our next party. – I'm sure she (be)

.... very happy when she (hear) .... this.

35. When my sister (see) .... my new hair cut, she (not believe) ....

.... her eyes.

36. Let's go before these idiots (come) .... back.

37. Sally, you (catch) .... a cold if you don't put on a coat. – Okay, Mum, I

(take) .... the fur coat I got for Christmas.

38. Don't worry about this rash. It (go) .... away soon.

39. Mrs. Wilson, (you, sit) .... here, please.

40. Mum has promised that she (write) .... to us as soon as she (arrive)

.... in Vienna.

41. Tom, you (not fool) .... me any longer. I know all your tricks.

42. If you bully me again, I (tell) .... my parents.

43. We (go) .... to the mountains on Saturday and Sunday. Do you want to

come with us ? – I'm sorry I can't. I'm helping my dad to build the new garage. Dad thinks we (be)

.... able to finish it this weekend.

44. What (your mum, say) .... when she hears about our engagement?

45. We (ask) .... Dad when he (get) .... home.

20 All types of "future" (will, going to, present simple, present progressive, future progressive): *Alle Typen der Zukunft (will, going to, present simple, present progressive, future progressive):*

1. Girls, (you, turn) .... down the radio, please? I'm thinking.
2. Look at the children, how peacefully they are playing. But in a little while they (fight) ...., like every day.
3. Why are you so nervous, Billy? – I think Mr. Nolan (ask) .... me to repeat the last lesson, and I'm not really prepared for it.
4. If the wind doesn't blow away the clouds, it (still, rain) .... tonight.
5. Why has your dad bought this long ladder? – He (fix) .... the roof.
6. You must try harder next time, Lucy, or you (fail) .... this semester.
7. Listen to this storm! It (knock) .... over the garden shed again.
8. I (leave) .... you now, but I hope you (still, wait) .... here when I get back in an hour or so.
9. Quick, do something! I can't control the fire. – I (get) .... the fire extinguisher!
10. The film was fantastic! People (still, talk) .... about it in ten years.
11. I can't find my sunglasses anywhere! – Don't worry, I (help) .... you to look for them. I'm sure together we (find) .... them very soon.
12. Do you know where I (be) .... tomorrow morning? I (sit) .... in an aeroplane to San Francisco. – Lucky you! When (you, return) ....? – I (probably, stay) .... for three weeks.
13. I know Julia is awful, but she (come) .... to party, if we like it or not.
14. Hurry up, Mum! The bus (leave) .... ten minutes from now!
15. If everything goes well, we (lie) .... on the beach this time next week.
16. Believe me, when we get home, the cat (sit) .... on the sofa again.
17. If we don't get there in time, they (shut) .... the doors before we (arrive) ....
18. Girls and boys, I (show) .... you a video about the natural wonders of Canada now. I hope you (enjoy) .... it.
19. You can protest as much as you like. Nobody (listen) .... to you.
20. If you don't listen to me, you (be) .... in deep trouble before you (know) .... it.
21. Have you heard? Rita (play) .... the cello at the concert next Sunday.
22. If I can, I (call) .... you before I (leave) ....

GERUND – "Gerund"

Das Gerund ist eine **ing-Form**. Es ist ein Zeitwort (Verb), das wie ein **Hauptwort (Nomen)** verwendet wird ("hauptwörtlich gebrauchtes Zeitwort").

Zur Erinnerung – die Bildung der "ing-Form":

• "Grundformel"	▶	*going, talking, helping, playing …*	→	Infinitiv + *ing*
• "Sonderformen"	▶	*ru**nn**ing, swi**mm**ing, sto**pp**ing …*	→	Verdoppelung des Mitlauts
		writing, taking, coming, losing …	→	Wegfall des *"e"*
		lying, tying, dying	→	*-ie* wird zu *-y*

Das Gerund wird verwendet …

(A) als **Subjekt** (meist ohne Artikel):
Skiing *is a lot of fun.* – ***The buying*** *and* ***selling*** *of drugs is illegal.*

(B) als **Prädikat oder Objekt:**
Look, it has stopped ***raining****.* – *We could hear* ***the crashing*** *of the waves.*

(C) nach bestimmten **Wörtern und Wendungen**:
The man admitted ***stealing*** *the money. – Joe is busy* ***studying*** *for the test.*

(D) anstelle bestimmter **Gliedsätze**:
After ***arriving*** *at the airport, we went to the check-in counter.*
(After we had arrived at the airport, …)

(E) Das Gerund **darf nicht** nach bestimmten Wörtern und Wendungen stehen.
Siehe dazu auch die Kapitel *"Infinitive"* (ab Seite 43) und *"Infinitive or Gerund"* (ab Seite 71).

21 Find the "ing-form" of the following verbs. *Bilde die "ing-Form" der folgenden Verben.*

1. answer ……………………………………………
2. break ……………………………………………
3. cut ……………………………………………
4. drive ……………………………………………
5. earn ……………………………………………
6. freeze ……………………………………………
7. get ……………………………………………
8. hide ……………………………………………
9. jump ……………………………………………
10. keep ……………………………………………
11. learn ……………………………………………
12. measure ……………………………………………
13. nod ……………………………………………
14. open ……………………………………………
15. print ……………………………………………
16. quarrel ……………………………………………
17. race ……………………………………………
18. stay ……………………………………………
19. try ……………………………………………
20. upload ……………………………………………
21. vary ……………………………………………
22. wake ……………………………………………
23. yield ……………………………………………
24. zip ……………………………………………

(A + B) GERUND AS SUBJECT, PREDICATE OR OBJECT

22 Translate the verbs and fill in the gerund.

Übersetze die Verben und setze sie als Gerund ein. Überlege, ob es sich um S, P oder O handelt.

1. (fahren) .... fast cars is a dangerous habit.
2. (lernen) .... an Eastern European language is getting very important.
3. (reparieren) .... a computer can sometimes be very difficult.
4. (spielen) .... computer games is often very exciting.
5. Long time (surfen) .... the internet can be very expensive.
6. (snowboarden) .... has become very popular among young people.
7. (anschauen) .... a Hitchcock film is always a great pleasure.
8. I hate people (rauchen) .... indoors.
9. Dad has always enjoyed (tun, machen) .... some sports in the evening.
10. Granny hates (bekommen) .... bad news.
11. (zeigen) .... violent films on TV should be forbidden.
12. I dislike (ausborgen) .... money.
13. Herbert gave up (um Geld spielen) .... when he grew older.
14. (arbeiten) .... hard is the key to success, they say.
15. Most people dislike (gehen) .... to the dentist.
16. Mum has often thought of (annehmen) .... a completely different job.
17. (sprechen) .... so much during the lecture was not very polite, Steve!
18. (leben) .... together with someone who snores is quite difficult.
19. In Ireland, (rauchen) .... is not allowed indoors.
20. Starting tomorrow, my brother will give up (rauchen) ....
21. (Schlittschuh laufen) .... on thin ice can be quite dangerous.
22. (lesen) .... good books can do you a lot of good.
23. Last night Dad was fined for (fahren) .... too fast in a built up area.
24. (zurückreden) .... to your parents is not a clever idea.
25. When they stopped (sprechen) .... at last, everybody was happy.
26. In London, we watched the (auswechseln, ablösen) .... of the Guard.
27. When did you start (malen) ...., Mr. Jones? – Two years ago.
28. Some people like (spazieren gehen) .... in the rain, but I don't.
29. (zuhören) .... to Max (erzählen) .... jokes is great fun.
30. I think I don't remember (sehen) .... you here before.

(C) GERUND AFTER CERTAIN VERBS AND PHRASES

(a) Gerund nach bestimmten Verben (Auswahl der wichtigsten):

admit	zugeben, gestehen	*Nobody **admits taking** the key.*
avoid	vermeiden	*We could not **avoid talking** to George today.*
consider	denken an, überlegen	*Have you ever **considered changing** school?*
(dis)like	(nicht) mögen	*I really **(dis)like doing** homework.*
enjoy	sehr gern tun/haben	*Did you **enjoy watching** the game?*
finish	beenden, fertigstellen	*Boys, **finish playing** and get back to work!*
forgive for	vergeben, verzeihen	*Please **forgive** me **for bothering** you, but ...*
imagine	(sich etwas) vorstellen	*Can you really **imagine winning** in the lottery?*
mention	erwähnen	*Did you **mention speaking** with Mrs. Robbins?*
mind	etwas dagegen haben	*We don't **mind** (your) **staying** a little longer.* *Do you **mind** (us) **shutting** the window?*
miss	vermissen, verpassen	*I **miss going** for walks with my dog.*
practise	üben, trainieren	*The coach said I must **practise catching**.*
risk	riskieren	*You'll **risk getting** fine if you drive so fast.*
suggest	vorschlagen	*Who **suggested walking** in this weather?*

23 Find the English verbs, fill in the gerund and translate the sentences into good German.
Finde die englischen Verben, setze sie als Gerund ein und übersetze die Sätze in gutes Deutsch.

1. The boy admitted (nehmen) .... a bar of chocolate and some chewing gum.
2. When the police asked the driver, he admitted (trinken) .... four beers.
3. Dad always avoids (waschen) .... his car himself. Then I have to do it.
4. Most pupils avoid (lernen) .... at the weekends.
5. If you can, avoid (werden) .... interviewed by the newspaper.
6. We did not go outside because we wanted to avoid (werden) .... wet.
7. A long time ago my grandparents considered (übersiedeln) .... into the city.
8. My parents are considering (verkaufen) .... our old car.
9. After our neighbours' cat had died, they considered (suchen) .... a new one.
10. Mum dislikes (aufstehen) .... so early in the morning.
11. Sally dislikes (aufräumen) .... her room.
12. My dad dislikes (essen) .... warmed up meals.
13. Uncle Harry enjoys (trinken) .... a glass of beer in the evening.
14. As Uncle Joe got older, he enjoyed (lesen) .... the Bible more and more.
15. As a boy, I always enjoyed (spielen) .... with Lego blocks.
16. Mum enjoys (arbeiten) .... in the garden.

17. Let's finish (tun, machen) .... our homework before Dad comes home.

18. When did you finish (anstreichen) .... the garden fence?

19. We finished (essen) .... dinner before the quiz show began.

20. I will never forgive you for (erzählen) .... my secret to everyone.

21. Forgive me for (anrufen) .... you so late, but it's important.

22. I can't imagine (ausgeben) .... so much money in such a short time.

23. Can you imagine (heiraten) .... somebody from a foreign country?

24. Tim often imagines (sein) .... a prince and (leben) ....

in a castle made of gold.

25. Imagine (gewinnen) .... a million Pounds. What would you do?

26. Did I mention (sehen) .... Prince Charles in London?

27. Our neighbours did not mention (besuchen) .... any museums in Madrid.

28. Dad never mentioned (nicht bestehen) .... any tests when he was in school.

29. The people did not mind (warten) .... outside.

30. Do you mind (abschalten) .... the radio while I am doing my homework?

31. Mum is not here right now. Do you mind (kommen) .... again tomorrow?

32. I wouldn't mind (füttern) .... your dog when you are on holiday.

33. We really missed (plaudern) .... with you while you were away.

34. I sometimes miss (lesen) .... my newspaper when I'm abroad.

35. Grandpa says that sometimes he misses (rauchen) .... his pipe after dinner.

36. Whenever I am away on holiday I miss (spielen) .... with my dog.

37. Professional musicians must practise (spielen) .... their instrument every day.

38. The whole class practised (tanzen) .... for the school ball.

39. You should always practise (lesen) .... aloud so that you can hear yourself.

40. Every day the boy practised (gehen) .... on his hands.

41. Don't hurry. You'll risk (stürzen) .... down the stairs.

42. If you eat so much, you risk (verlieren) .... your shape.

43. The company will risk (gehen) .... bankrupt if they spend so much on ads.

44. As we got closer to the city, Mum suggested (fahren) .... a bit slower.

45. I suggested (bestellen) .... baked beans for breakfast.

46. The waiter suggested (geben) .... some ketchup on the hamburger.

47. Forgive me for (fragen) ...., but would you consider (verkaufen)

.... your car? – No, I still enjoy (fahren) .... it a lot!

48. When Uncle Max bought the factory, he risked (verlieren) .... everything.

(b) Gerund nach bestimmten Fügungen mit *"to be"* + *adjective* + *preposition*
(Auswahl der wichtigsten):

to be afraid of	sich vor etwas fürchten, Angst haben	*Linda is **afraid of fighting.***
to be capable of	zu etwas fähig / in der Lage sein	*I'm not **capable of lying.***
to be far from	weit davon entfernt sein, etwas zu tun	*He's **far from believing** us.*
to be fond of	etwas gerne tun/haben	*Sue is **fond of dancing.***
to be good at	bei/in etwas gut sein	*Tim is very **good at skiing.***
to be interested in	an etwas interessiert sein, sich für etwas interessieren	*We are **interested in seeing** your new photos.*
to be proud of	auf etwas stolz sein	*Are you **proud of winning?***
to be responsible for	für etwas verantwortlich sein, schuld sein an etwas	*Who is **responsible for opening** the windows?*
to be surprised at	von/über etwas überrascht sein	*I'm **surprised at seeing** you.*
to be tired of	etwas satt haben / genug haben	*We're **tired of waiting.***
to be tired from	von etwas müde sein	*He's **tired from running.***
to be used to	an etwas gewöhnt sein	*They are **used to hearing** strange stories.*

24 Find the English verbs, fill in "preposition + gerund" and translate the sentences into good German.

Finde die englischen Verben, setze "Präposition + Gerund" ein und übersetze die Sätze in gutes Deutsch.

example: Dad was afraid (verlieren) too much money, so he stopped gambling. ▶
Dad was afraid *of losing* too much money, so he stopped gambling.
Vater hatte Angst, zu viel Geld zu verlieren; also hörte er mit dem Spielen auf.

1. Sally was afraid (bekommen) .... bad marks, so she didn't take the test.
2. Not many people thought that we were capable (gewinnen) .... the match.
3. The two old ladies were far (sein) .... rich, but they took part in the auction.
4. My daughter is really fond (spielen) .... the cello, so she practises very hard.
5. Mum is good (beruhigen) .... me down when I'm nervous.
6. Most girls are interested (lesen) .... about music and fashion.
7. Max was proud (beenden) .... first in the quiz.
8. One teacher was responsible (unterrichten) .... more than fifty pupils.
9. We were surprised (sehen) .... our friends in such an expensive restaurant.
10. I went to bed because I was tired (arbeiten) .... hard all day.
11. The burglars were afraid (werden) .... caught by the police, so they ran away.
12. Mum is not used (essen) .... so much in the evening.

13. Shut up, boys! I'm tired (anhören) .... to all this nonsense!

14. Don't try to fool me! Are you capable (machen, tun) .... the job or aren't you?

15. As Robert was not used (leben) .... alone, he moved back to his parents.

16. Mum was interested (lernen) .... an exotic language, so she took Swahili.

17. Our teacher is good at Maths, but she is not good (erklären) .... it to us.

18. After two hours the boys were tired (lernen) .... irregular verbs for the test, so they watched TV instead.

19. At some parties even the boys are fond (tanzen) ....

20. Ian is very proud (kennen) .... Sean Connery personally.

21. It's really true, my dog is capable (verstehen) .... more than fifty words.

22. Mr. Lee wants to know who is responsible (reinigen) .... the board this week.

23. After the weekend, some teachers are tired (verbessern) .... tests and essays.

24. Mark has always been good (singen) ...., so he is studying music.

25. Walter is such an egoist. He's not used (zuhören) .... to anybody but himself.

26. The police were surprised (finden) .... the money in the woman's house.

27. Only two men were responsible (zählen) .... the votes.

28. The old people say that the young are not used (arbeiten) .... hard any more.

29. Mum was tired (kochen) .... for so many people, so she took a rest.

30. After his wife had left him, Mr. Trask saw that he was not capable (tun) .... all the work in the house by himself.

31. As I was not interested (schauen) .... TV any more, I turned it off.

32. I was far (gewinnen) .... the race, but I enjoyed it very much and I was really proud (beenden) .... it.

33. Granny is fond (backen) .... cakes, so we get a cake every other day.

34. Rich people are more interested (verdienen) .... money more than (ausgeben) .... it.

35. This book is far (sein) .... Hohlbein's best, but I like it.

36. I'll speak with Miss Myers. I'm not afraid (erzählen) .... her what has happened.

37. You shouldn't be proud (essen) .... so many hotdogs. That's not healthy!

38. You're really fond (sich lustig machen) .... of other people, aren't you?

39. Are you good (zuhören) ...., boys? I'd like to tell you a story.

40. My sister has always been capable (erfinden) .... interesting excuses.

41. We were not really surprised (nicht bestehen) .... the test.

42. VIPs are not used (warten) .... in shops or restaurants.

(c) Gerund nach bestimmten Fügungen mit *verb + preposition*
(Auswahl der wichtigsten):

to apologise for	sich entschuldigen	*Vic **apologized for forgetting** the book.*
to believe in	überzeugt sein von, glauben an	*I **believe in helping** people in need.*
to depend on	abhängen von	*My happiness **depends on having** friends.*
to feel like	zumute sein nach	*Do you **feel like staying** or **going**?*
to give up	aufgeben, aufhören	*Never **give up trying** to do better!*
to go/keep on	weitermachen	***Go/Keep on running**! Don't stop now!*
to insist on	bestehen auf	*Dad **insists on going** to work today.*
to keep from	abhalten von	*You can't **keep** me **from going** home.*
to prevent from	hindern an	*You can't **prevent** me **from going** home.*
to look forward to	sich freuen auf	*I'm **looking forward to visiting** you soon.*
to put off	verschieben	*Don't **put off doing** your homework again!*
to succeed in	gelingen	*Joe **succeeded in solving** the problem.*
to talk about/of	von/über etwas sprechen	*Don't **talk about/of leaving** now.*
to thank for	(sich be)danken für	*Bob **thanked** me **for helping** him.*
to think about/of	an/über etwas (nach)denken	*Do you ever **think about buying** a new car?*
to worry about	sich um etwas sorgen	*I never **worry about getting** bad marks.*

25 **Find the English verbs, fill in "preposition + gerund" and translate the sentences into good German.**
Finde die englischen Verben, setze "Präposition + Gerund" ein und übersetze die Sätze in gutes Deutsch.

example: My parents gave (fahren) their motorbikes many years ago. ▶
My parents *gave up riding* their motorbikes many years ago.
Meine Eltern gaben das Motorradfahren vor vielen Jahren auf.

1. Dad apologised (verwenden) .... my PC, but his did not work.
2. My dad believes (sagen) .... what he thinks.
3. Police work depends (bekommen) .... all kinds of information.
4. My brother often does not feel (gehen) .... to school, so he stays at home.
5. After losing again, Mike Tyson gave (boxen) ....
6. You must go (spielen) .... the violin, or you won't pass your exam.
7. Joe kept (schauen) .... TV long after the others had gone to bed.
8. Dave insisted (tragen) .... his old jeans to the party.
9. Bungee jumping is dangerous, but you can't keep me (versuchen) .... it.
10. We were looking forward (sehen) .... our cousins again after five years.
11. A policeman tried to prevent the man (springen) .... out of the window.
12. As Sally had a bad cold, we put (besuchen) .... our grandparents.

13. Magicians usually succeed (überraschen) .... their audiences.

14. My parents have always been talking (machen) .... a journey to the USA.

15. Our teachers believe (arbeiten) .... together with us pupils.

16. Most tests depend (sein) .... well prepared and well organised.

17. I did not feel (gehen) .... out, so I stayed at home and read a book.

18. The teacher insisted (überprüfen) .... our bags before the test.

19. We couldn't keep Alex (schwimmen) .... in the ice-cold water.

20. Most girls look forward (gehen) .... out as soon as they are old enough.

21. We were looking forward (besuchen) .... Madame Tussaud's in London.

22. When my dad was young, he was thinking (werden) .... a soccer professional.

23. Mum sometimes talks (geben) .... her diamond earrings away.

24. Tony kept (zurückreden) .... to the teacher until she became angry.

25. Dad always insists (haben) .... the last word.

26. You can try to keep me (gehen) .... to the party, but it won't work.

27. Are you looking forward (reisen) .... to Australia this summer?

28. We did everything to prevent Tina (hören) .... about Mike's accident.

29. When Jim said he was busy, we put (besuchen) .... the picture show.

30. I'm sure you will succeed (finden) .... a good job soon.

31. When will you stop talking (verlieren) .... the match?

32. I don't believe (bitten) .... other people for help all the time.

33. Getting a good job sometimes depends (kennen) .... the right people.

34. Do you feel (reden) .... about your problems with me?

35. Sir, this gentleman insists (sprechen) .... with you personally.

36. We tried to keep Joe (geraten) .... into trouble, but it was no good.

37. I used to look forward (werden) .... older, but now I'm not so sure any more.

38. We always look forward (besuchen) .... new countries in our holidays.

39. Dad says he is thinking (verkaufen) .... the car and (kaufen)
.... a bigger one.

40. Whenever we go out with our grandparents, they insist (bezahlen) .... for us.

41. Jenny has called three times today, but I don't feel (reden) .... with her.

42. Sometimes I worry (nicht finden) .... a good job after school.

43. Have you succeeded (kontaktieren) .... your parents, Joe? – No, not yet.

44. You always talk (einladen) .... me to one of your parties, but you never do.

45. We are all looking forward (machen, tun) .... some crazy things this summer.

(d) Gerund nach bestimmten Redewendungen (*"phrases"*)
(Auswahl der wichtigsten):

to be busy	mit etwas beschäftigt sein, eifrig dabei sein	*Eric **is busy writing.***
cannot help could not help	nicht anders können, einfach etwas tun müssen	*We **couldn't help laughing.***
cannot stand could not stand	nicht ausstehen können, nicht ertragen können	***I can't stand dancing.***
it's no good it's no/little use	es hat keinen Sinn, es hat wenig Sinn	***It's no good talking** to her. **It's no use asking** her now.*
it's (not) worth	es ist es (nicht) wert	*London **is worth visiting.***
What about ...? How about ...?	Was ist mit ...? Wie wär's mit ...?	***What about having** lunch? **How about staying** here?*

26 Find the English verbs, fill in the gerund and translate the sentences into good German.

Finde die englischen Verben, setze das "Gerund" ein und übersetze die Sätze in gutes Deutsch.

1. How about (gehen) ....for a walk?
2. It's no use (beginnen) .... now; it's still too cold outside.
3. I can't help (lächeln) .... when I see Bill and Mary together.
4. Don't buy this book. It's not worth (lesen) ....
5. Let's do something! I can't stand (tun) .... nothing all day!
6. I believe it's little use (sprechen) .... with Jim. He won't help us.
7. Tom can't talk to you. He is busy (vorbereiten) .... for the final game.
8. Forget Gerry! He's not worth (weinen) .... about!
9. What about (bitten) .... your dad for help?
10. I can't help (sein) .... angry and sad when I hear the news.
11. Let's call a taxi. It's no use (versuchen) .... to start the car.
12. When I looked at the photos, I couldn't help (denken) .... of last summer.
13. How about (einladen) .... the neighbours to a barbecue tonight?
14. It's no good (pflanzen) .... flowers now. It's too late in the year for it.
15. When my mum was a girl, she couldn't stand (gehen) .... to kindergarden.
16. Please switch off the radio. I can't stand (anhören) .... to this music.
17. When I came to school this morning, everybody was busy (lesen) ....
18. They say Manhattan is fantastic. – Yes, it's really worth (sehen) ....
19. Can you come or are you busy (machen, tun) .... something?
20. What about (sagen) .... us the truth?

(e) Gerund nach *"without"* und *"instead of"*:

without	ohne ... zu	*They left the bar **without paying**.*
instead of	(an)statt ... zu	*Joe watched TV **instead of going** to bed.*

27 Find the English verbs, fill in the gerund and translate the sentences into good German.
Finde die englischen Verben, setze das "Gerund" ein und übersetze die Sätze in gutes Deutsch.

1. Sally rode home on the bike instead of (warten) .... for her brother.
2. Dad tried to repair the car himself instead of (bringen) .... it to the garage.
3. Instead of (stehen) .... around and (tun) .... nothing, David wanted to help.
4. Instead of (gehen) .... home, Sabrina took a taxi.
5. You could ask your teacher instead of (reden) .... with your classmates.
6. We wanted to go to a restaurant instead of (kochen) .... for ourselves.
7. Instead of (kaufen) .... a new car, the Jacksons made a holiday in Jamaica.
8. Instead of (färben) .... her hair, Linda got it cut very short.
9. Dad bought me a new bike instead of (reparieren) .... the old one.
10. Instead of (gehen) .... home, Bernie stayed at the fun park with his friends.
11. You should save some money instead of (ausgeben) .... it all on silly things.
12. Mary left the room angrily instead of (warten) .... for an explanation.
13. Lena was so tired that she went to bed without (putzen) .... her teeth.
14. You should never enter a room without (anklopfen) ....
15. I'm not going to leave Paris without (sehen) .... Leonardo's Mona Lisa.
16. Without (fragen) ...., Kevin took my bike and rode off.
17. I don't want to say what I think without (reden) .... to the people first.
18. The girl ran across the street without (schauen) .... right or left.
19. Simon sold his mountain bike without (fragen) .... his parents.
20. Eddie jumped into the water without (denken) .... of the consequences.
21. The burglar opened the door without (verwenden) .... a key.
22. My grandma never goes to bed without (sagen) .... a prayer.
23. Without (üben) .... every day you won't become perfect.
24. The men ran over red hot coals without (verletzen) .... themselves.
25. Dad never leaves the house in the morning without (küssen) .... Mum.
26. Joe solved the problem himself instead of (bitten) .... someone for help.

28 Translate the sentences into good English, using the words and phrases of (A), (B) and (C).

Übersetze die Sätze in gutes Englisch; verwende die Wörter und Wendungen von (A), (B) und (C).

1. Lauf weiter! Das Rennen ist noch nicht vorüber.
2. Ich kann mir nicht vorstellen, in dieses Haus einzuziehen.
3. Bitte sag nichts davon (= erwähne es nicht), dass du mich hier gesehen hast.
4. Der Mann gab zu, die Frau zu kennen.
5. Wir können es nicht riskieren, den Test zu versäumen.
6. Sabrina vermeidet es, mit Dennis auszugehen.
7. Unsere Nachbarn überlegen, ihr Haus zu verkaufen und wegzuziehen.
8. Ich werde nie zugeben, dass ich das Spiel verloren habe.
9. Helen spricht immer davon, eine bekannte Sängerin zu werden.
10. Oma macht gerne ein Nachmittagsschläfchen.
11. Mein Vater ist es gewöhnt, die ganze Nacht zu arbeiten.
12. Fritz mag es nicht, wenn er warten muss.
13. Die Soldaten waren müde vom langen Marschieren.
14. Kluge Menschen vermeiden es, in Schwierigkeiten zu geraten.
15. Arthur entschuldigte sich dafür, dass er die Vase kaputt gemacht hatte.
16. Könntest du dir vorstellen, den ganzen Weg zu Fuß zu gehen?
17. Wir freuen uns darauf, den Urlaub in Tirol zu verbringen.
18. Judy ist stolz darauf, dass sie die Beste in ihrer Mannschaft ist.
19. Brian fährt gerne mit seinem neuen Auto herum.
20. Ich habe es wirklich satt, mir eure Ausreden anzuhören.
21. Harry bestand darauf, mir sein neues Zimmer zu zeigen.
22. Wir waren überrascht, Martha mit Andy zu sehen.
23. Okay, ihr habt gewonnen! Ich gebe es auf, mit euch zu streiten.
24. Es interessiert mich nicht, die alten Geschichten zu hören.
25. Glaubst du, Olivia ist in der Lage, das Rätsel zu lösen?
26. Ich bin weit davon entfernt, dir zu glauben.
27. Wir möchten uns dafür entschuldigen, dass wir während deiner Rede gelacht haben.
28. Anne kann sehr gut mit Kindern arbeiten.
29. Die Kinder sind es nicht gewöhnt, so spät schlafen zu gehen.
30. Bitte sprich weiter. Ich höre dir gerne zu.
31. Mr. Nelson bestand darauf, mich nachhause zu fahren.
32. Meine Eltern haben nie daran gedacht, aufs Land zu ziehen.
33. Hast du jemals daran gedacht, in einem Chor zu singen?
34. Du hast nie erwähnt, dass du Fisch nicht magst.
35. Hat es dich gestört, dass du warten musstest?
36. Mir macht harte Arbeit nichts aus.
37. Ich schlage vor, wir bestellen zwei große Pizzen.
38. Du solltest trainieren, schlimme Dinge zu vergessen.
39. Ich vermisse es wirklich, euch zuzuhören.
40. Tom schlug vor, den Direktor um Erlaubnis zu fragen.
41. Vor ein paar Jahren las ich gerne die Bücher von Thomas Brezina.

42. Wer ist für das Geschirrwaschen verantwortlich?
43. Ich gehe gern mit meinen Freunden weg.
44. Wann werdet ihr aufhören, mir auf die Nerven zu gehen?
45. Kannst du mir verzeihen, dass ich dich belogen habe?
46. Fred gab zu, dass er sich geirrt hatte.
47. Hör auf mit dem Jammern und tu etwas!
48. Es macht uns nichts aus, mit den Besuchern Englisch zu sprechen.
49. Lydia vermisst die Besuche bei ihren Freundinnen.
50. Frank möchte nicht riskieren, Elisabeth zu verlieren.
51. Nach dem Unfall musste Joe wieder Gehen üben.
52. Du hast nicht erwähnt, dass du mit Monica gesprochen hast.
53. Wir können es nicht riskieren, Mr. Berger zornig zu machen.
54. Ein Baseballspieler muss oft Fangen und Schlagen üben.
55. Wir haben es verpasst, uns die Ausstellung anzuschauen.
56. Macht es dir etwas aus, heute länger zu arbeiten?
57. Vermeide es, mit Gus zu sprechen, wenn er nervös ist.
58. Wir hörten um 10 Uhr mit dem Tanzen auf.
59. Bitte verzeih mir, dass ich den ganzen Kuchen gegessen habe.
60. Warum hast du zugegeben, dass du das Fahrrad genommen hast?
61. Kannst du dir vorstellen, mit mir in einer Klasse zu sein?
62. Ich spreche nicht gerne über andere Leute.
63. Wenn du mit dem Packen fertig bist, können wir fahren (*leave*).
64. Habe ich erwähnt, dass ich Dorothy angerufen habe?
65. Ich schlage vor, dass wir heute Abend Monopoly spielen.
66. Wir haben nichts dagegen, dass wir jetzt anfangen.
67. Wir haben es verpasst, mit Joe zu sprechen, so lange er hier war.
68. Es hat keinen Sinn zu weinen.
69. Ich bin nicht imstande, die Frage zu beantworten.
70. Julia gibt gerne Partys.
71. Verena kann sehr gut zeichnen (= sie ist darin sehr gut).
72. Pamela hatte Angst davor, allein durch den Park zu gehen.
73. Brad Pitt hatte es satt, die Fragen der Reporter zu beantworten.
74. Niemand kann uns davon abhalten, heute Abend ins Kino zu gehen.
75. Mir ist heute nach Singen und Tanzen zumute.
76. Ich kann es nicht ertragen, mit dummen Menschen zu arbeiten.
77. Ich möchte dir für deine Hilfe danken.
78. Erik macht sich immer Sorgen, dass er seinen Busausweis verliert.
79. Gerry fuhr mit dem Bus nachhause, anstatt auf seine Mutter zu warten.
80. Ich verlasse diesen Raum nicht, ohne vorher mit Mr. Smith zu sprechen!
81. Wir konnten Großvater nicht daran hindern, den alten Traktor zu verkaufen.
82. Da ich Fieber hatte, mussten wir den Zoobesuch verschieben.
83. Schreib weiter, bis du keine Fehler mehr machst.
84. Danke, dass du heute mit dem Hund spazieren gehst.
85. Das Ende des Films war so traurig, dass ich weinen musste.

(D) GERUND CONNECTS AND SHORTENS SENTENCES

(Gerund anstelle bestimmter Gliedsätze zum Verbinden und Verkürzen von Sätzen)

(a) *"after" – "before" – "when"* ▶ Zeitsätze (wann?)

after	▶	*after*	*After we left the cinema, we went to McDonald's.* ***After leaving** the cinema, we went to McDonald's.*
before	▶	*before*	*Before Tina went to bed, she switched off the lights.* ***Before going to** bed, Tina switched off the lights.*
when	▶	*on*	*When Dad opened the garage, he noticed a strange smell.* ***On opening** the garage, Dad noticed a strange smell.*

▶▶▶ VORAUSSETZUNG: gleiches Subjekt in Hauptsatz und Gliedsatz

(b) *"by" + gerund* ▶ Modalsätze (wie?)

Asafa Powell broke the world record. He ran the 100 m in 9.77 seconds.
*Asafa Powell broke the world record **by running** the 100 m in 9.77 seconds.*

If you look to the right, you can see the Matterhorn.
***By looking** to the right, you can see the Matterhorn.*

▶▶▶ VORAUSSETZUNG: gleiches Subjekt in beiden Sätzen

29 Shorten these sentences with the help of a gerund.

Verkürze die Sätze mit Hilfe eines "Gerunds".

1. When I saw the photos of Tina and myself, I couldn't help laughing.
2. Sam usually says a prayer before he writes an exam.
3. Before you go to Julia's place, call and ask if she's at home.
4. I usually read a book three or four times before I give it away.
5. After Dad had lost the shopping list, he did not know what to buy.
6. When Samantha saw the slug in her salad, she fainted.
7. Before I open a letter or a parcel, I always look at the sender.
8. When Beatrice heard the results of her exam, she had tears in her eyes.
9. Before I look out of the window, I always turn off the lights.
10. After Theo had closed the door of the secret room, he lit a candle.
11. When Lydia comes home after work, she makes herself a cup of tea.
12. Before we go upstairs, we always check all the doors downstairs.
13. Dad usually kisses Mum good-bye before he leaves for work in the morning.
14. After the men had paid for their drinks, they left the bar.
15. The men left the bar before they had paid for their drinks.
16. When we opened the front door, we saw a strange sight.
17. The postman rang the doorbell a couple of times before he pushed the telegram under the door.

18. After Aunt Helen had opened her shop, she waited for the first customers.
19. When Fred saw Georgina for the first time, he fell in love with her.
20. Before the guest opened the newspaper, he ordered a cup of coffee.
21. When our history teacher comes into the classroom, she always smiles at the pupils.
22. When we read the article in the newspaper, we finally found out the truth about the fight.
23. I was very tired after I had painted the garden shed.
24. Before Dad answered my question, he thought carefully for a minute.
25. After Dave had lost the tennis match, he walked home sadly.
26. When Mum returned from walking the dog, she found a message on the answerphone.
27. She fed the dog before she listened to the message on the phone.
28. Before Mr. Wilson sent us home, he declared the meeting over.
29. Dorothy's little brother got sick after he had eaten a grasshopper.
30. When I see a teacher in town, I avoid looking at him or her.
31. Before Maria gets into the car, she always crosses herself.
32. After Farmer Jones had fed the cows, he looked after the pigs.
33. Jenny played the piano before she studied the guitar.
34. When Mrs. Banks saw the broken window, she informed the police.
35. After Grandpa finished digging the garden, he sat down and smoked his pipe.
36. We found a nice hotel after we had checked with the tourist information.
37. Before I can say yes or no, I must know more about the problem.
38. After I had heard about Molly's accident, I decided to call her.
39. When Joe returned from his adventure holidays, he had a lot to tell.
40. You should check the conditions before you sign anything.
41. Mr. Togger had a mysterious disease after he came back from the tropics.
42. After she had seen a documentary about animal transports, Daisy decided to become a vegetarian.
43. When Uncle Will heard of my interest in animals, he invited me to stay at his farm.
44. Before you ask another question, think about the problem for a moment.
45. Sherpa Tensing became very famous after he had climbed Mt. Everest.
46. Sometimes, when I wake up in the middle of the night, I don't know where I am.
47. After Lord Cavendish had welcomed the guests, he showed them around the castle.
48. Before you touch anything in this room, you should ask for permission.
49. We were very depressed when we heard the results of the exam.
50. Our neighbours lived in Germany and Italy before they moved to our town.
51. Jack had no money left after he had bought the laptop.
52. Before Dad leaves the house, he always looks at the thermometre.
53. When we arrived at the youth hostel, we phoned our parents.
54. Bettina did not like Peter very much before she got to know him better.
55. After they had talked for a while, they decided to go to the cinema on Saturday.
56. Richard had known Ina for three years before he asked her to marry him.
57. After she had said yes to Richard, Ina was very happy.
58. After Manuel had punched David in the face, he was sent to the headmaster.
59. Before the boys went home, they put away all the toys.
60. When Simon saw what he had done, he was very sorry.
61. Some kids are very tired after they finish this exercise.

30 Connect or shorten these sentences with the help of a gerund.

Verbinde oder verkürze die Sätze mit Hilfe eines "Gerunds".

1. Alan solved the problem. He spoke about it with his father.
2. The police caught the thieves. They checked all the customers in the shop.
3. Sally changed her looks. She dyed her hair pink.
4. Columbus sailed west. He wanted to reach India.
5. Toby answered all the questions correctly. He won the quiz.
6. Max showed us his new mountain bike. He wanted to impress us.
7. The prisoners escaped from jail. They dug a tunnel under the wall.
8. The burglars got into the house. They climbed up the drain pipe.
9. The old lady drove off the mugger. She hit him with her handbag.
10. Tony pretended to be ill. He avoided taking the test.
11. Dad took a taxi. He got to the airport in time.
12. Daniel studied harder than ever before. He finally got good marks.
13. The magician made himself invisible. He put on a black cloak.
14. Mum got well again. She took her pills regularly.
15. Dad used his credit card. He opened the door of our hotel room.
16. (after a plane crash in the desert) The pilot survived. He stayed near the wreck until help arrived.
17. We got tickets for the concert. We ordered them on the internet.
18. Mum gained three kilos over Christmas. She ate too many sweet things.
19. Martin prepares for the marathon. He runs twenty kilometres every other day.
20. Many people tried to help the victims of the tsunami. They gave money to aid organisations.
21. Roald Amundsen beat Robert Scott by a few days. He was the first man on the South Pole.
22. Brazil won the World Cup again. They won nine out of ten matches.
23. They saved the girl's life. They pulled her out of the water.
24. The shop assistant pressed the alarm button. He informed the police of the robbery.
25. Joe makes some extra money. He delivers newspapers on Sunday.
26. Alice let me use her cell phone. She saved me from a lot of trouble.
27. Gina copied from Teresa. She got an "A" on her French test.
28. Tony set off the alarm. He touched one of the objects at the exhibition.
29. If you do what I say, you will save us a lot of work.
30. If you follow the route on the map, you will find the house easily.
31. You will lose 50 pounds in three months if you follow this new diet.
32. You will improve your knowledge of foreign languages if you work abroad for a while.
33. If you insulate your house, you can save a lot of money.
34. If you drive at night, you can avoid traffic jams.
35. We would save time and money if we stayed at home.
36. You would know more about the history of this place if you watched this film.
37. If we used solar energy instead of coal and oil, we could protect the environment better.
38. If you had asked the people for the way, you would have got there in time.
39. In the USA you can call the police, the ambulance or the fire brigade if you dial 911.
40. Today you can get a lot of information quickly if you use the internet.
41. If you stay at campgrounds and youth hostels, you can see the world cheaply.

INFINITIVE – Infinitiv, Nennform

Der Infinitiv ist die **erste Stammform** des Verbs. Er wird **mit und ohne *"to"*** verwendet.

Den Infinitiv verwendet man …

(A) nach bestimmten Zeitwörtern *(verbs)* ▶ ***verb + infinitive***
*The boys **decided to go** to the sports centre.*
*I'm sorry, but I **cannot help** you.*

(B) nach Eigenschaftswörtern *(adjectives)* ▶ ***adjective + infinitive***
*We are **sad to hear** that you did not enjoy your holidays.*

(C) nach bestimmten Hauptwörtern *(nouns)* ▶ ***noun + infinitive***
*You have no **right to say** such things about me!*

(D) nach Fragewörtern *(question words)* ▶ ***question word + infinitive***
*Sam did not know **what to do** in this situation.*

(E) nach ***first, last, best, only*** … ▶ ***"extreme word" + infinitive***
*Mr. Lee is usually the first to arrive in the morning and the **last to leave** at night.*

(F) nach ***"too + adjective"*** und ***"enough + noun"***
Rebecca is so young that she can't remember the flood of 1997.
*Rebecca is **too young to remember** the flood of 1997.*

This is so much wood that we can build two tree houses.
*This is **enough wood to build** two tree houses.*

(G) Der Infinitiv **darf nicht** nach bestimmten Wörtern und Wendungen stehen.
Siehe dazu auch die Kapitel "*Gerund*" (Seite 28) und *"ing form" or infinitive?* (Seite 71).

(A) VERB + INFINITIVE

(a) Verben, die *"infinitive with to"* verlangen (Auswahl):

afford	sich etwas leisten	*Let's walk! We can't **afford to take** a taxi.*
agree	zustimmen, dafür sein	*Harry **agreed to help** me.*
allow	erlauben	*Who has **allowed** you **to leave** the room?*
ask	bitten	*We have **asked** Joe **to come** with us.*
attempt	versuchen	*The stranger **attempted to sell** us some books.*
decide	beschließen, entscheiden	*Dad **decided to visit** his old friends in England.*
expect	erwarten	*I did not **expect to see** you here.*
happen	(zufällig)	*Columbus **happened to find** a new continent.*
hesitate	zögern	*Mike **hesitated to lend** me his books.*
hope	hoffen	*We **hope to hear** from you soon.*
learn	lernen	*Frank **learned to ride** a bike when he was three.*
manage	gelingen, schaffen	*I **managed to do** everything best.*
offer	anbieten	*Helen **offered to feed** the cat when we are gone.*
plan	planen, beabsichtigen	*Tom and Sue **are planning to get** married soon.*
pretend	vortäuschen, so tun … als ob	*Gina **pretended to like** me.*
promise	versprechen	*You **promised to play** chess with me, Dad!*
refuse	ablehnen, sich weigern	*I **refuse to believe** this nonsense.*
seem	scheinen	*The baby **seems to like** me!*
want	wollen	*Who **wants to go** swimming today?*
wish	wünschen	*We **wish to know** more about the accident.*

31 Find the English verbs and fill in the infinitive (with "to").

Setze das passende englische Verb im Infinitiv ein (mit "to").

1. I have really enjoyed talking to you. I hope (sehen) .... you again very soon.
2. Bernie has lost my pen, but he promised (kaufen) .... me a new one.
3. Do you want (essen) .... now or later? – Later. I'm not hungry yet.
4. We must win the next match. We absolutely can't afford (verlieren) .... it.
5. Lord Cavendish was very kind. He offered (zeigen) .... us the castle himself.
6. I refuse (arbeiten) .... with you if you don't show more enthusiasm.
7. If you happen (sprechen) .... with Erica, tell her to call me or send me an e-mail.
8. What's the matter, Dominique? You seem (sein) .... depressed about something.
9. What do you expect (tun) .... in Washington? – Well, we want (besuchen) .... all the important places.
10. I told Dad that I wanted (kaufen) .... a new bike, and he agreed (leihen) .... me half of the money.
11. Jackie is so lazy! She never manages (beenden) .... her projects in time.
12. Ben decided (bitten) .... Laura for a date. He wanted (gehen) .... to the cinema with him.
13. Sandra is learning (spielen) .... the violin together with her brother. They are planning (beitreten) .... the school orchestra.
14. I wanted (sehen) .... the new "Star Wars" film, but my friends didn't want to go.
15. I promised my sister (senden) .... her a letter as soon as I got to London.
16. My father refused (bezahlen) .... the bill, as he did not get what he had wanted.
17. I happened (treffen) .... my English teacher at the concert last Saturday.
18. Time seems (vergehen) .... quickly when you are in nice company.
19. We can't afford (machen) .... our teachers angry. They are in a better position.
20. Some old people wish (sein) .... young again.
21. The man did not hesitate (erzählen) .... the police what he had seen and heard.
22. They attempted (brechen) .... the world record, but they did not make it.
23. Our town fathers are planning (bauen) .... a fifth bridge across the river.
24. You seem (verstecken) .... something from us. Why don't you tell us everything?
25. When I was young, I wanted (werden) .... a famous pop star.
26. The boys decided (anrufen) .... their parents and tell them what had happened.
27. I happened (hören) .... what you were saying, and I absolutely refuse (glauben) .... this story.

28. We did not expect (gewinnen) .... so much money.

29. Everybody hoped (bekommen) .... tickets for the concert, but they were sold out.

30. Paul promised not (ausgeben) .... so much money on computer games in future.

31. They asked the doctor not (kommen) .... again the next day.

32. The headmaster agreed (erlauben) .... the older students (smoke) .... outside the school building.

33. The clown didn't want (sagen) .... us how he did the trick.

34. The old man offered (aufpassen) .... our bikes while we were inside the shop.

35. Mum refused (backen) .... another cake for the party.

36. The boys asked their teacher (zeigen) .... them how to do the homework.

37. Sally offered (aufräumen) .... her brother's room if he cleaned her boots.

38. Herman hesitated (geben) .... us his cell phone number.

39. Thanks for your visit. We hope (sehen) .... you again soon.

40. All the doors were locked, but we managed (klettern) .... in through a window.

41. Mum has decided not (verkaufen) .... her car now. She wants (fahren) .... it for another year or two.

42. Monica is happy because Bill has promised (anrufen) .... her soon.

43. Mike, I wish (sprechen) .... about your school report with you. Now!

44. Look at the birds! They seem (fliegen) .... away for the winter.

45. Dad pretended (schlafen) .... but in fact he was listening to the radio.

46. Mr. Myers seems (verdienen) .... a lot of money. Just look at his house!

47. Who happens (sich erinnern) .... Jessica's phone number?

48. Martina and Chris expected (hören) .... from us, but we forgot to write.

49. Kevin is really mean. He offered not (erzählen) .... the teachers about the broken window if I promised (schenken) .... him my MP3 player.

50. The government attempted (verbieten) .... fox hunting, but the people were against it. So the government agreed (erlauben) .... it for two more seasons.

51. We didn't expect (hören) .... from you so soon, but we are delighted about it.

52. Mark is still very weak after his illness, but he hopes (sich erholen) .... soon.

53. Dad and his brothers are planning (überraschen) .... their parents this Christmas.

54. Joe pretended (gehen) .... away, but he hid behind the door.

55. Caroline offered (geben) .... me maths lessons before the next test.

56. Look at this ruin! I'm sure they will decide (niederreißen) .... one of these days.

57. My grandparents have decided (verkaufen) .... their business.

32 Translate into good English, using the words from the box.

Übersetze in gutes Englisch, indem du die Wörter aus dem Rahmen verwendest.

afford – agree – allow – ask – attempt – decide – expect – hestitate – hope – learn – manage – offer – plan – pretend – promise – refuse – seem – want – wish

1. Es gelang mir, die anderen zu überzeugen.
2. Du musst versprechen, dass du diese Geschichte vergisst!
3. Schau dir den Hund an! Er scheint das Wasser zu genießen.
4. Können wir es uns leisten, heuer auf Winterurlaub zu fahren?
5. Immer mehr Menschen weigern sich, Fleisch zu essen.
6. Mr. Brown stimmte zu, die Polizei zu informieren.
7. Wir beschlossen, Brian im Spital zu besuchen.
8. Wir hoffen, euch nächstes Jahr wieder zu sehen.
9. Ich erwarte nicht, dass ich dieses Jahr Probleme in der Schule haben werde.
10. Wir haben vor (= wir planen), bis Sonntag hier zu bleiben.
11. Dad, wo hast du Auto fahren gelernt?
12. Unsere Nachbarn boten an, die Blumen auf der Terrasse zu gießen.
13. Ich verspreche, dass ich das Geld morgen zurückzahle.
14. Joe gab vor, Kopfweh zu haben.
15. Dem Vogel gelang es, sein Nest auf der Spitze des Baumes zu bauen.
16. Dave und Sally beschlossen, ihre Nachbarn zu Weihnachten einzuladen.
17. Die Klasse plante, mit dem Boot den See zu überqueren und am Ufer wieder zurückzuwandern.
18. Olivia lehnte es ab, den Brief zu lesen.
19. Großvater versprach, bald wieder zu kommen.
20. Du scheinst Schifahren zu mögen.
21. Der Feuerwehr gelang es, das Kätzchen vom Baum zu holen.
22. Ich wünsche, mit deinen Eltern zu sprechen.
23. Kannst du es dir leisten, so ein teures Fahrrad zu kaufen?
24. Nancy lehnte es ab, mit Alex auf die Party zu gehen.
25. Meine Freunde hoffen, dass sie dieses Jahr mit ihrer Klasse nach England fahren.
26. Die Kandidaten stimmten zu, den Wettbewerb zu beenden.
27. Sie beschlossen, den Wettbewerb im kommenden Jahr zu wiederholen.
28. Voriges Jahr planten wir, euch zu unserer Feier einzuladen, aber dann wurde sie verschoben.
29. Wir erwarteten, dass wir die Bücher heute bekommen.
30. Die Frau tat so, als ob sie mich kannte, aber sie hatte keine Idee, wer ich war.
31. Ein Hund muss lernen, seinem Herrn zu gehorchen.
32. Der Doktor bot an, am Abend wieder zu kommen.
33. Er wollte den Patienten noch einmal untersuchen.
34. Sie versprach ihrem Bruder, ihm die CD morgen zurückzugeben.
35. Die Männer erlaubten uns, auf den Caterpillar zu klettern.
36. Die beiden Buben weigerten sich, mit dem Hund spazieren zu gehen.
37. Ich bat Mr. Conrad, die Frage zu wiederholen.
38. Die Gefangenen versuchten zu entkommen.
39. Zögere nicht, mich anzurufen, wenn du Hilfe brauchst.

(b) Verben, die *"infinitive without to"* verlangen (Auswahl):

- ***modal verbs*** ▶ ***can(not), may (not), must (not), will (not), shall (not), need (not)***
  *Steven **may come** to the party or he **may not come**; I don't know.*

- **Verben der Sinneswahrnehmung*** ▶ ***see, hear, watch, feel****
  (wenn es immer, oft, nie ... so ist/war)
  *Every night we **hear** the milk truck **drive** past our house.*
  *Diese Wörter treten auch mit *"present participle"* auf. (Siehe dazu auch Seite 64.)

- **nach *"let"* und *"make"*** ▶ **in der Bedeutung von "lassen", "veranlassen"**
  *Dad sometimes **lets** me **drive** the car.* (Er erlaubt es.)
  *Mum always **makes** us **do** the shopping.* (Sie veranlasst es.)

- **nach *"had better (not)"* und *"had rather (not)"*** ▶ **"sollte/würde lieber"**
  *We'**d better go** now or we'll miss the last train.*
  *I'm tired, so I'**d rather not play** tennis today.*

- **nach der Aufforderung *"why not?"*** ▶ **"(Mach) doch ...!"**
  ***Why not ask** Miss Jones for help?* → Bitten wir doch Miss Jones ...!

33 Find the English verbs and fill in the infinitive (without "to").

Setze das passende englische Verb im Infinitiv ein (ohne "to").

1. They always meet here at this time. I can see them (gehen) .... into the house.
2. They did not let us (verwenden) .... our dictionaries, so there will be mistakes.
3. Look at the clock! We'd better (aufhören) .... at once or we'll be late again.
4. Shall I (legen) .... the books on the table or on the shelf? – On the table, please.
5. I'd rather (machen) .... a bike tour than (gehen) .... to school.
6. Bill, I think I heard someone (rufen) .... your name. – That was probably Mum.
7. We wanted to go out last night, but Dad made us (bleiben) .... at home and (lernen) .... for the test today.
8. I don't want to watch TV now. I'd rather (gehen) .... for a walk with my dog.
9. Tim's dog is chasing your cat again, Joe. You'd better (rufen) .... him back.
10. Our neighbours are very nice. They often let us (schwimmen) .... in their pool.
11. I'm sorry, but there's nothing I can (tun) .... about this situation.
12. Tea or coffee, Veronica? – I'd rather (haben) .... a glass of milk, please.
13. When I come home from school, I can (riechen) .... lunch from the kitchen.
14. I like to feel the wind (wehen) .... into my face.
15. From my window I see the deer (kommen) .... out of the forest to feed.
16. George didn't let me (abschreiben) .... his homework.

17. At the weekends we need not (aufstehen) .... so early in the morning.

18. I'd rather (schreiben) .... a German test than an English test.

19. Mr. Hopkins made me (bleiben) .... after school although I hadn't done anything.

20. You must (abgeben) .... your portfolios next Friday.

21. When I fall asleep, I can feel my arms (werden) .... heavier and heavier.

22. You must not (vergessen) .... your books again.

23. We watched the birds (fliegen) .... away for the winter.

24. The film made her (weinen) .... like a baby.

25. You had better not (essen) .... so much in the evening or you will (have) .... nightmares in your sleep.

26. You needn't (machen) .... everything alone, Grandma. I'll help you.

27. You must not (überqueren) .... the street against the red light.

28. In the evening you can watch the fog (kommen) .... in from the sea.

29. You had better (anziehen) .... a warm coat on such a cold day.

30. Can you (reichen) .... me the salt, please?

31. Don't let your dog (laufen) .... around in the streets.

32. Every afternoon we hear Julian (spielen) .... the piano for an hour.

33. You'd better (waschen) .... your hands before dinner.

34. Believe me, I can make the car (fahren) .... much faster.

35. The Holy Bible says, "You shall not (stehlen) ....!"

36. I don't like Jim, so I'd rather not (einladen) .... him to my party.

37. Mum made Dad (nehmen) .... dancing lessons with her. He hated it!

38. Fred, you'd better (tun) .... something about your cold! It's getting worse.

39. Our English teacher makes us (lernen) .... lots of new words every lesson.

40. We'd better (beeilen) .... or Mum will be angry with us.

41. Every Sunday I hear my neighbour (kommen) .... home early in the morning.

42. They didn't let us (verlassen) .... the room during the exam.

43. Sir, we'd rather (spielen) .... basketball than football.

44. You'd better not (zurückreden) .... to Mr. Walker. He can get very angry!

45. Remember, you must not (öffnen) .... the letter before Sunday!

46. You can't make me (tun, machen) .... it if I don't want to!

47. I think we'd better (warten) .... for Chuck and Lisa before we start.

48. Why not (versuchen) .... something new this time?

34 Translate into good English, using the infinitive without "to".

Übersetze in gutes Englisch mit Hilfe des Infinitivs ohne "to".

1. Ich würde heute lieber ins Kino gehen.
2. Sie haben uns die Fotos nicht anschauen lassen.
3. Wir sollten jetzt lieber gehen.
4. Soll ich dich morgen anrufen?
5. Wir würden im Sommer lieber nach Griechenland fahren als nach Spanien.
6. Hast du jemand aus dem Haus kommen gesehen?
7. Mr. Trask ließ uns die Übung zweimal schreiben.
8. Schauen wir den Buben beim Fußballspielen zu!
9. Dad ist böse. Wir sollten ihm lieber alles erzählen.
10. Simon ist in Ordnung. Er lässt uns manchmal auf seiner Play Station spielen.
11. Es tut mir leid, aber es gibt nichts, was ich gegen diese Situation tun kann.
12. Kann ich etwas für dich tun?
13. Ein Urlaub in Österreich lässt Sie Ihre Sorgen vergessen!
14. Wir hören Flora oft singen, während sie duscht.
15. Mutter hat uns die Geschenke nicht vor Weihnachten öffnen lassen.
16. Wir müssen die Geschichte nicht bis morgen schreiben.
17. Du solltest jetzt lieber schlafen gehen.
18. Sie ließen uns so viel essen, wie wir wollten.
19. "Romeo and Juliet" ließ mich zu einem Fan von Leonardo DiCaprio werden.
20. Du solltest nicht so viel Unsinn daherreden.
21. Ihr könnt nicht erwarten, dass ich euch immer helfe.
22. Müssen wir wirklich alle Übungen machen?
23. Wir hören die Leute über uns jeden Abend streiten.
24. In Großbritannien müssen Autos auf der linken Straßenseite fahren.
25. Im Herbst fühlt man, wie die Nächte kühler werden.
26. Du solltest lieber einen Regenschirm mitnehmen.
27. Kannst du mir bitte das Fernsehprogramm mitnehmen?
28. Lass deinen Hund nicht auf der Straße herumlaufen.
29. Ich höre euch oft gemeinsam singen.
30. Ihr solltet euch vor dem Schlafengehen duschen.
31. Unser Lehrer sagt, er kann uns nachsitzen lassen, wenn er will.
32. Du darfst nicht alles glauben, was in der Zeitung steht.
33. Ich sah, wie die Männer um 8 Uhr das Haus betraten und wie sie es eine Stunde später verließen.
34. Man ließ uns das Video nicht anschauen.
35. Der Polizist veranlasste die Menschen, weiterzugehen.
36. Trinken wir doch eine Tasse Kaffee, bevor wir nachhause gehen.
37. Die alte Dame möchte ihr Haus jetzt lieber nicht verkaufen.
38. Du musst nicht den ganzen Preis auf einmal bezahlen.
39. Gehen wir doch spazieren, so lange die Sonne scheint.
40. Sag Larry, er soll sich lieber beeilen.
41. Schauen wir uns doch gemeinsam ein Video an.

35 Find the English verbs and fill in the infinitive (with or without "to").

Setze das passende englische Verb im Infinitiv ein (mit oder ohne "to").

1. I am sorry (enttäuschen) .... you but we cannot (machen) .... it your way.
2. You needn't (kommen) .... to my place today. I'd rather (beenden) .... some work for tomorrow.
3. I asked my friends not (erzählen) .... their parents about the last weekend, but they refused (zuhören) ....
4. You seem (kennen) .... the town quite well, Jack. – That's because I used (wohnen) .... here for a while when I was young.
5. I'd rather (stay) .... at home than (ausgehen) ....
6. You can't (lassen) .... your dog here with us because we don't want (haben) .... an animal in our house.
7. If you don't want (helfen) .... me in the kitchen, you needn't (kommen) .... to my place at all.
8. When would you like (essen = haben) .... breakfast, Dave? – At 8.30, please.
9. The teacher let the boys (gehen) .... home earlier, because he wanted (treffen) .... his girlfriend.
10. You'd better (schicken) .... me an email soon if you decide (gehen) .... camping with us.
11. I offered (tragen) .... Carrie's books so that I could (kennen lernen) .... her better.
12. Naomi Campbell made the audience (warten) .... for hours, but then she agreed (posieren) .... for pictures.
13. I'll let you (wissen) .... my answer as soon as I know it myself.
14. We expect (treffen) .... Jonathan in Dublin next week.
15. My German teacher refuses (akzeptieren) .... printouts from the internet.
16. You shouldn't let the child (spielen) .... with your mobile phone.
17. Teenagers must learn (sagen) .... no to drugs.
18. I'm planning (haben) .... my own business when I'm thirty.
19. They asked me (warten) .... longer than I had planned (warten) ...., but then they offered (geben) .... me the job.
20. You needn't (warten) .... for me. I'll manage (finden) .... the way without you.

21. Grandma never lets us (gehen = weggehen) .... without a little present.
22. I promise (schicken) .... you the photos as soon as possible.
23. You'd better (sagen) .... me your address. Perhaps I'll (schreiben) .... you a postcard.
24. If you want (kommen) .... home before dark, you'd better (werden) .... ready now.
25. You needn't (fragen) .... me if you want (holen) .... something from the fridge.
26. In kindergarden they made us (verwenden) .... knives and forks instead of a spoons.
27. The teacher let us (denken) .... about the problem for as long as we wanted.
28. Foreign tourists often wish (besuchen) .... only the famous sights of a city.
29. There's nothing wrong with my ears, so you needn't (schreien) .... !
30. Just look into my eyes and you will (wissen) .... what I mean.
31. You have (sein) .... quiet now, children. Dad is talking on the phone.
32. I did not expect (finden) .... anyone here. The house seemed (sein) .... empty.
33. You'd better (laufen) .... if you want (erreichen) .... the bus.
34. They made us (singen) .... the whole song five times.
35. Josephine refused (lernen) .... the text of the song, but she promised (spielen) .... the tune on her guitar.
36. Mrs. Foley seemed (sein) .... in a good mood, so she pretended (forget) .... yesterday's homework.
37. Every Friday Mum makes us (aufräumen) .... our rooms.
38. We can hear the dogs (bellen) .... all night. It's so noisy sometimes that we can't (schlafen) ....
39. When Debbie was a little girl, she often watched her mum (auftragen) .... her make up. Later on she attempted (nachahmen) .... her.
40. I promised my parents (füttern) .... the goldfish every week.
41. Mum allowed me (einladen) .... twenty people to my party.
42. I watched the car (anhalten) .... in front of our house and two men (aussteigen) ....
43. James never learned (lesen) .... music, but he managed (bestehen) .... the exam at the music academy.
44. Hermione decided (erzählen) .... Harry and Ron everything she had found out.

(c) *"verb + object + infinitive"*

- ***verb + object + infinitive*** ▶ **wie auf Deutsch**

The general	***ordered***	***his troops***	***to attack.***	→ **mit *"to"***
Der General	befahl	seinen Truppen	anzugreifen.	
Dad often	***lets***	***me***	***use*** *the car.*	→ **ohne *"to"***
Vater	lässt	mich	das Auto verwenden.	
	verb +	*object* +	*infinitive*	

- ***verb + object + infinitive*** ▶ **statt eines "dass"-Satzes**

Julia	***wants***	***us***	***to help*** *her in the kitchen.*
	verb +	*object* +	*infinitive*
Julia	möchte,	dass wir ihr in der Küche helfen.	

Geeignete Verben für *"verb + object + infinitive"* sind:

advise	(be)raten, einen Rat geben	*What can you **advise me to do** now?*
allow	gestatten, erlauben	*Mum doesn't **allow us to stay out** late.*
ask	bitten, ersuchen	*Can I **ask you to hold** this for a minute, please?*
expect	erwarten	*We **expect them to do** their job well.*
help	helfen	*Dad often **helps me to solve** Maths problems.*
invite	einladen, auffordern	*I'd like to **invite you to sing** in our choir.*
know	wissen, kennen (als)	*You **know me to work** hard.*
order	befehlen	*They **ordered us to stay** inside.*
remind	(jemand) erinnern	*You don't always have to **remind me to feed** the dog.*
teach (how)	lehren, beibringen	*Let's **teach the boys how to put up** a tent.* *Who **taught you to speak** Spanish so well?*
tell	sagen, befehlen	*We **told them to be** quiet.*
want	wollen, mögen	*I **want you to listen** to me carefully.*
wish	wünschen, wollen	*Sue **wished Tom to go out** with her.*
would like	mögen, wollen	*They **would like him to join** their team.*

36 Translate into good English with the help of "verb + object + infinitive".

Übersetze in gutes Englisch mit Hilfe von "verb + object + infinitive".

1. Judith bat mich, ihre Einkaufstasche zu tragen.
2. Niemand erlaubte uns, den Raum zu betreten.
3. Meine Eltern raten mir oft, mehr für die Schule zu tun.
4. Ich half meinem Bruder, sein Fahrrad zu reparieren.
5. Onkel Fred hat uns eingeladen, die Ferien auf seinem Boot zu verbringen.
6. Der Direktor befahl den Schülern, die Graffiti zu übermalen.
7. Joe erinnerte mich daran, die Bücher zurückzubringen.
8. Mein Vater brachte mir bei, auf den Händen zu gehen.
9. Meine Eltern erwarten, dass ich Arzt oder Anwalt werde.
10. Ich möchte, dass du noch einen Tag bleibst.

11. Wir wissen, dass Michelle eine gute Schülerin ist.
12. Jeder sagt mir, ich solle eine Instrument spielen lernen.
13. Laura hätte gern, dass ich mit ihr auf den Ball gehe.
14. Wer hat gesagt, ihr sollt aufhören?
15. Ich wollte nicht, dass du das weißt.
16. Mrs. Snider bat mich, den Brief für sie aufzugeben.
17. Grandma erlaubt uns nicht, dass wir gehen, ohne eine Stück Kuchen zu probieren.
18. Ich erwarte, dass ihr alle hart arbeitet.
19. Julia wollte, dass ich mir ihr neues Zimmer anschaue.
20. Peter möchte, dass wir ihn am Sonntag besuchen.
21. Meine Oma erinnerte mich daran, ein Geschenk für Mutter zu kaufen.
22. Mr. Graham gestattete uns, auf seiner Wiese Fußball zu spielen.
23. Wir kennen Sabine als ausgezeichnete Tänzerin. (= Wir wissen, dass sie ... ist.)
24. Vater sagte, wir sollten unser Zimmer aufräumen.
25. Ich möchte nicht, dass du heute noch weggehst.
26. Mrs. Feinstein befahl Martin, das Geld sofort zurückzugeben.
27. Viele Männer erwarten, dass ihre Frauen jeden Tag für sie kochen.
28. Ich wünsche, dass ihr alle diesen Artikel lest.
29. Stephanie möchte nicht, dass Alex mit ihr tanzt.
30. Jenny bat mich, ihre Eltern zu verständigen.
31. Mr. Tompkins bat mich, die Zeitung für ihn zu holen.
32. Das Publikum erwartet, dass alle Schauspieler ihr Bestes geben.
33. Die Leute im Zug sagten, wir sollten ruhig sein.
34. Ich möchte, dass ihr zu meinem Geburtstagsfest kommt.
35. Meine Eltern erlaubten mir, eine Woche lang mit meinen Freunden herumzureisen.
36. Tante Alice bat mich, sie zu begleiten.
37. Großmutter erwartet, dass wir sie am Wochenende besuchen.
38. Soll ich dir ein Geheimnis erzählen? (= Möchtest du, dass ich ... erzähle?)
39. Unsere Lehrer erwarten, dass wir die Hausübungen sorgfältig machen.
40. Hast du gewollt, das Victor ins Kino mitgeht?
41. Wir ließen es nicht zu, dass die Gäste zu laut wurden.
42. Ich möchte nicht, dass jemand im Haus raucht.
43. Wir wissen, dass du Tiere magst.
44. Sie sagten uns, wir sollten morgen wiederkommen.
45. Joe bat mich, ihm etwas Geld zu borgen.
46. Ich möchte dir raten, vorsichtiger zu sein.
47. Wir hätten es nicht gerne, wenn Gertrud davon erfährt.
48. Dr. Brown half mir, wieder gesund zu werden.
49. Die Soldaten befahlen den Menschen, ihr Dorf zu verlassen.
50. Meine Nachbarin hat mir beigebracht, wie man kocht.
51. Wir wissen, dass du Briefmarken sammelst.
52. Sabrina bat mich, sie an den Test zu erinnern.
53. Ich möchte nicht, dass du mit meiner Freundin sprichst.
54. Soll ich dir mein Fotoalbum zeigen? (= Möchtest du, dass ich ... zeige?)

37 Translate into good English with the help of "verb + object + infinitive".

Übersetze in gutes Englisch mit Hilfe von "verb + object + infinitive".

1. Ich wünsche, dass du mir von dem Vorfall erzählst.
2. Mr. Smith erlaubt uns, fünf Minuten vor Ende der Stunde wegzugehen.
3. Wir sehen sie immer um Mitternacht heimkommen.
4. Dominic wollte, dass ich ihn besuche.
5. Der Lehrer bat uns, etwas lauter zu sprechen.
6. Unsere Eltern erlaubten uns nicht, dass wir ins Kino gingen.
7. Die alte Mrs. Robinson schaut den Buben immer beim Basketballspielen zu.
8. Tom bat mich, ihn zum Bahnhof zu bringen.
9. Vater sagte meinen Freunden, sie sollten im Haus nicht rauchen.
10. Ich wollte nicht, dass wir zu spät kamen.
11. Jack erwartet, dass wir pünktlich sind.
12. Claudia wollte, dass Tobias mit ihr kommt.
13. Patrick möchte, dass wir ihm am Wochenende helfen.
14. Bitte erinnere mich, dass ich dir die neue CD borge.
15. Mrs. Wilson erlaubte mir nicht, über ihr Feld zu gehen.
16. Kevin soll ein sehr guter Sänger sein. (Wir wissen, dass ...)
17. Mutter trug uns auf, das Aquarium zu putzen.
18. Mr. Stellar wollte nicht, dass wir diese Datei öffnen.
19. Mama wünscht sich, dass wir heute früher schlafen gehen.
20. Deborah befahl David, dass er sie in Ruhe lassen solle.
21. Eine Frau erwartet, dass der Mann sie beschützt.
22. Ich möchte nicht, dass jemand während der Schularbeit spricht.
23. David erinnerte seine Schwester daran, ihre Eltern anzurufen.
24. Ich höre oft, dass sich meine Freunde über die Schule beklagen.
25. Der Mann bat mich, sofort den Arzt zu verständigen.
26. Ich habe nicht erwartet, dass ihr so viel Geld bei euch habt.
27. Mein Großvater riet mir, nur Mineralwasser zu trinken.
28. Wir müssen den Menschen beibringen, sich selbst zu helfen.
29. Die Leute im Park sagten, wir sollten nicht so viel Lärm machen.
30. Kann mir jemand helfen, die Pakete ins Haus zu tragen?
31. Johns Eltern erlauben ihm, dass er den ganzen Abend ausbleibt.
32. Ich hätte gern, dass du bei mir bleibst.
33. Vater brachte mir bei, wie man Bäume setzt.
34. Der Polizist befahl uns, den Kofferraum zu öffnen.
35. Ich sagte Mario, er solle mir morgen meine Bücher zurückgeben.
36. Anne bat uns, auf sie zu warten.
37. Ich möchte nicht, dass du so viel rauchst.
38. Wir hatten erwartet, dass uns Mr. Higgins einladen würde.
39. Wir alle wissen, dass Kriege schrecklich sind.
40. Ich wünsche, dass ihr mir zuhört.
41. Wir hatten nicht erwartet, dass sich das Wetter so rasch ändern würde.

(B) ADJECTIVE + INFINITIVE

Chinese is ***difficult to write.***
We were ***sad to see*** *you go.*
That's not ***easy to believe.***

▼ ▼

adjective + infinitive

38 Fill in the English words (adjective + infinitive) and translate into German.

Setze die passenden englischen Wörter ein (adjective + infinitive) und übersetzte in gutes Deutsch.

1. It's not (*leicht zu wissen*) .... what children want for Christmas.
2. I was very (*froh zu sehen*) .... you again so soon.
3. This text is really (*schwer zu verstehen*) ....
4. It's (*unmöglich zu finden*) .... the correct answer.
5. Nobody was (*traurig zu hören*) .... that Joe couldn't come.
6. It was (*schön zu erhalten*) .... the photos.
7. I think it is (*angenehm zu leben*) .... in Germany or Austria.
8. We should be (*froh zu genießen*) .... freedom and peace.
9. Susan, are you (*bereit zu beginnen*) .... ?
10. It's not (*in Ordnung zu nennen*) .... someone an idiot.
11. It's (*schwer zu verstehen*) .... why you don't like Sabrina.
12. I think it's not (*notwendig zu kaufen*) .... a laptop.
13. Dominic was very (*enttäuscht zu bekommen*) .... a "C".
14. It's (*wichtig sich zu erinnern*) .... this date: October 24, 1947.
15. Sam was (*überrascht zu lesen*) .... my e-mail.
16. Do you think it's (*möglich zu sprechen*) .... with your parents?
17. It's always (*gut zu haben*) .... a real friend.
18. It's not (*ungewöhnlich zu sehen*) .... eagles in the mountains.
19. Is it (*gefährlich hinaufzuklettern*) .... the ladder?
20. Tom was (*schockiert zu entdecken*) .... that his cat was dead.
21. It's (*unhöflich zu betreten*) .... a room without saying hello.
22. I'm (*neugierig herauszufinden*) .... who won the first prize.
23. Dad says it's (*wichtig zu kennen*) .... the right people.
24. It is (*nicht erlaubt zu spielen*) .... football on the lawn.
25. The people were (*glücklich zu überleben [sie hatten Glück]*) .... the crash of their plane.

39 Shorten or connect these sentences, using "adjective + infinitive".

Verkürze die folgenden Sätze mit Hilfe von "adjective + infinitive".

example: Dad is sorry that he will miss the match tonight. ▶
Dad is *sorry to miss* the match tonight.

1. Sue was very happy that she got an "A" in English.
2. We were sorry when we heard about your stolen bike.
3. Gerry was glad when he got Michelle's letter.
4. I was lucky that I found my passport again.
5. We were not surprised when we heard that you couldn't come to the party.
6. You should be happy that you have friends like us.
7. Bob, are you ready? Can we go?
8. Peter was shocked when he found the knife in his drawer.
9. We were satisfied when we passed the exam.
10. I'm not happy that I'm here today.
11. Aren't you glad? You'll move into a bigger house soon.
12. George is sad that he has to leave us next week.
13. You are lucky that you are unhurt.
14. It is important that you remember the password.
15. The children are ready. They can go to bed.
16. I feel honoured that I can speak at the conference.
17. Carrie must be crazy if she sells her house now.
18. We are sorry that we must tell you this.

40 Translate into English, using "adjective + infinitive".

Übersetze mit Hilfe von "adjective + infinitive" in gutes Englisch.

1. Es war wichtig, über das Problem zu sprechen.
2. Wir fühlen uns geehrt, heute Abend hier zu sein.
3. Es tut mir leid, dass ich Sie stören muss.
4. Es ist nicht nötig, jede Frage zu beantworten.
5. Ich war zufrieden, eine positive Antwort zu bekommen.
6. Es ist nicht lustig, ein Spiel zu verlieren.
7. Es war großartig, euch wiederzusehen.
8. Joe hatte Glück. Er erreichte den letzten Bus.
9. Es war nicht leicht, das richtige Haus zu finden.
10. Es tut uns leid, dass wir euch enttäuschen müssen.
11. Es ist normal, dass man nach einem Spaziergang hungrig ist.
12. Ich war froh, von meinen Freunden Post zu bekommen.
13. Es würde mich freuen, Ihnen die Stadt zu zeigen.
14. Bist du bereit? Kannst du über den Unfall sprechen?
15. Du solltest froh sein, Mr. Strong als Lehrer zu haben.
16. Dieses physikalische Phänomen ist schwer zu erklären.
17. Manchmal ist es leicht, an Wunder zu glauben.
18. Es ist gefährlich, mit vollem Magen ins Wasser zu springen.

(C) NOUN + INFINITIVE

Eine Reihe von Hauptwörtern (Nomen) verlangen den Infinitiv mit *"to"*.
Dazu zählen die folgenden Wörter (Auswahl der wichtigsten):

ability	Fähigkeit	*Human beings have the **ability to speak**.*
chance	Gelegenheit, Chance	*This is your **chance to become** famous.*
opportunity	Möglichkeit	*Everyone has the **opportunity to become** rich.*
command ***order***	Befehl	*The general gave the **command to attack**.* *Our **orders** are **not to let** anyone pass through here.*
courage	Mut	*Nobody had the **courage to stop** the thieves.*
decision	Entscheidung	*It's your **decision to stay** or **to go**.*
freedom	Freiheit	*In Austria we have the **freedom to say** what we like.*
permission	Erlaubnis	*The pilot asked for **permission to land**.*
possibility	Möglichkeit	*Is there a **possibility to find** work in this town?*
reason	Grund	*There is **reason to believe** that the men are lying.*
right	Recht	*Go away! You have no **right to be** here!*
time	Zeit	*It was **time to say** good-bye.*
way	Art, Weise	*Frank has a **way to make** people laugh.*
wish	Wunsch	*Is it really your **wish to sell** the house?*

41 Translate into English, using "noun + infinitive".

Übersetze mit Hilfe von "noun + infinitive" in gutes Englisch.

1. Ich habe nicht den Mut, meinen Eltern alles zu erzählen.
2. Mein Vater hat die Fähigkeit, sofort einzuschlafen.
3. Das ist deine Chance, eine Menge Geld zu verdienen.
4. Dies ist nicht die Art, wie man Freunde gewinnt.
5. Es war Großvaters Wunsch, noch einmal das Meer zu sehen.
6. Tut mir leid, aber es Zeit zum Nach-Hause-Gehen.
7. Es ist unser Recht, auf diesem Land zu wohnen.
8. Beruhige dich, Jane! Das ist kein Grund zum Nervöswerden.
9. Deine Entscheidung, deine Eltern zu fragen, war in Ordnung.
10. Man gab uns die Erlaubnis, das Gebäude zu betreten.
11. Morgen hast du die Gelegenheit, die Rolling Stones live zu sehen.
12. Manche Tiere haben die Fähigkeit, bei Nacht zu sehen.
13. Olivers größter Wunsch ist es, Pamela Anderson kennen zu lernen.
14. Beeile dich! Das ist deine Chance, mit Pamela zu sprechen.
15. Ist das deine Art, über einen Freund zu sprechen?
16. Wir bieten Ihnen die Möglichkeit, das Auto eine ganze Woche lang zu testen.
17. Ich habe jetzt keine Zeit zum Nachdenken.
18. Die Polizisten warteten auf den Befehl zum Stürmen des Hauses.
19. Jason hatte den Mut, mir von seiner Tat zu erzählen.
20. Ihr habt kein Recht, so von mir zu sprechen.
21. Wessen Entscheidung war es, hier anzuhalten?
22. Ich habe keinen Grund, an deinen Worten zu zweifeln.
23. Wenn du älter bist, hast du die Freiheit zu tun, was du willst.

(D) QUESTION WORD + INFINITIVE

- eine sehr elegante und typisch englische Art, einen Satz kurz und bündig zu halten
- ersetzt einen Gliedsatz*

Nobody told me	***where***		***to put***	*the books.*
I have no idea	***who***		***to ask***	*about the exam results.*
Do you know	***how***		***to find***	*this address?*
Some people don't know	***when***		***to stop***	.
Have you decided	***what***	*clothes*	***to wear***	*to the party?*
Can you tell me	***which***	*bus*	***to take***	*to Victoria Station?*
	▼		▼	
	question word	+	***infinitive***	

*anstelle von: *Nobody told me where I should put the books.*
I have no idea who I could ask about the exam results.
Do you know how we can find this address?
Some people don't know when they should stop.
Have you decided what clothes you will wear to the party?
Can you tell me which bus I must take to Victoria Station?

42 Shorten these sentences, using "question word + infinitive".

Verkürze die folgenden Sätze mit Hilfe von "question word + infinitive".

1. The boys did not know what they should do with the baby hedgehog.
2. The tourist asked me how he could get to the science museum.
3. They told me what songs I should sing for my grandparents.
4. Tom is terrible. He doesn't know how he should behave in a restaurant.
5. Sally asked her mum which dress she should wear for her summer ball.
6. We wanted to know where we should sit at the concert.
7. They did not tell us who we should greet first.
8. I did not ask how much I should pay for the CD.
9. They did not think about where they had to go, they just went on.
10. The little boy did not know why he had to sit still during the performance.
11. Who knows where we must pay for the things?
12. Can you tell me when we should be there?
13. I asked myself how I should answer so many questions in fifteen minutes.
14. Cynthia had forgotten where she should get off the train.
15. Sandra could not remember who she could ask for advice.
16. Who showed you how you must do this?
17. The girls were not sure what they should say.
18. We had no idea how we should react in this situation.
19. It was hard to decide when we should stop.
20. The people wondered where they should go.
21. Tom was sure who he could ask for help.
22. I didn't know where I should start.
23. The boss showed me how I had to do the job.

24. The burglar did not know where he should hide the stolen things.
25. In a police state it's difficult to know who you can trust.
26. The hikers were not sure where they should cross the river.
27. Dad couldn't make up his mind where he should hide the Easter eggs.
28. My parents hardly knew what they should tell us children.
29. Gina was so shocked that she didn't know where she should run.
30. Sometimes I don't know what I can believe.
31. I can tell you how you can say this in Spanish.
32. Can you show me where I should start looking?
33. We don't know which CDs we should bring to the party.
34. I've no idea where I should start looking.
35. I never know what presents I should buy.
36. Do you remember how this word is pronounced correctly?
37. Helen wants to find out when she should start cooking.
38. Dad is wondering where he should build the garden shed.
39. Do you know what you can feed the little dog?
40. Can you tell me where I must change trains?
41. A friendly woman showed me how bread is made the old way.
42. In the summer holidays I sometimes don't know what I shall do in my spare time.
43. Do you always know what you should tell your parents?
44. Have you decided when you will start with the project?
45. Somebody please tell me when I must stop!
46. Denise never knows how far she can go.
47. Claire sometimes forgets when she should keep her mouth shut.
48. Andrea can show you how one paints with water colours.
49. Fiona is always uncertain what shoes she should wear in winter.
50. The driving instructor will tell you when you can go and when you must stop.
51. They say swimming is easy, but nobody could teach me how I had to do it correctly.
52. Do you have any idea what subjects you will take next year?
53. The tourist information suggested where we could get typical souvenirs.
54. A brochure explained how we should put the bookshelf together.
55. There was a plan in every room that showed what we should do in case of a fire.
56. The plan also told us who we should call and what number we should dial.
57. There can be no question how you should behave as a group.
58. I've told you many times what you can do and what you can't do.
59. Conrad wants to know what he should do with the empty boxes.
60. I think you can show him where he should put them.
61. The Math teacher explained how we could solve the problem.
62. Grandma can never remember where she must get on and off the bus.
63. The manual did not say how we could program the computer.
64. You did not tell us when we should pick you up.
65. Joe, do you know who you can ask if you have a problem?
66. Ernesto, can you show us how one dances the tango?

(E) "EXTREME WORD" + INFINITIVE

Die so genannten ***"extreme words"*** umfassen

- **Ordnungszahlwörter**
  first, second …
- **Superlative**
  last, best …
- ***"the only"***

Die Fügung ***extreme word + infinitive*** dient zum **Verkürzen** und **"Veredeln"** von Sätzen:

Neil Armstrong was the first man who set foot on the moon.
▶ *Neil Armstrong was **the first to set** foot on the moon.*

Number 1 was easier to answer than all other questions.
▶ *Number 1 was **the easiest** question **to answer.***

Billy Elliot was the only boy who attended the ballet class.
▶ *Billy Elliot was **the only** boy **to attend** the ballet class.*

43 Shorten these sentences, using "extreme word + infinitive".

Verkürze die folgenden Sätze mit Hilfe von "extreme word + infinitive".

1. My neighbour was the only one who survived the accident.
2. It would be best if you called a doctor, I think.
3. Alex, you are the second athlete who finished in under ten minutes. How do you feel now?
4. I'm sure Mr. Franklin is the best man that you could ask for advice.
5. My group was the only one that lost all their games.
6. Miss Jones, you were the last person that saw Billy. When was that?
7. You are always the last person that starts work and the first person that goes home again.
8. Jack, the only thing you can do now is to apologise.
9. In the story, David Copperfield is the only boy who asks for more food.
10. It is more difficult to find pink pearls than other pearls.
11. I was the first boy in my class who saw the new biology teacher.
12. The old man was the last person that got on the bus.
13. Opening the door was the worst thing that you could do at that moment.
14. My dad is usually the only one that drinks beer.
15. It would be best if we stopped at the next restaurant.
16. Our teachers were the first who told us the truth about the incident.
17. My brother was the last person that understood the problem.
18. I was the only one at my table that ordered rice with the fish.
19. The best drink that goes with steak is beer.
20. The worst thing that you can do is to drink and drive.
21. The thirteenth person that calls will win a prize.
22. "No" is the only answer that you can expect in this situation.
23. The English were the first who used steam engines in their coal mines.
24. I feel I'm always the last who knows what's going on.
25. Do you want to be the next that get their hair cut?
26. At 77, John Glenn was the oldest astronaut that went into space.

(F) "TOO + ADJECTIVE" & "ENOUGH + NOUN" WITH THE INFINITIVE

So lassen sich Sätze verkürzen oder verbinden und stilistisch verbessern:

After the match I was so tired that I didn't go out with my friends.
▶ *After the match I was* ***too tired to go out*** *with my friends.*

Joe had so much money that he paid for our tickets, too.
▶ *Joe had* ***enough money to pay*** *for our tickets, too.*

44 Shorten these sentences, using "too + adjective" and "enough + noun" with the infinitive.
Verkürze die folgenden Sätze mit Hilfe von ***"too + adjective"*** *und* ***"enough + noun"*** *und dem Infinitiv.*

1. The tea was so hot that we could not drink it.
2. The trousers were so small that they didn't fit me.
3. The car is so unsafe that we don't drive it any more.
4. It was so loud in the room that we did not understand a word.
5. The kids were so small that they could not reach the light switch.
6. The thieves were so clever that the police could not catch them for a long time.
7. The night was so dark that we did not see anything.
8. Jack was so nervous that he could not concentrate.
9. The refugees were so weak that they could not walk any further.
10. Jessica is so clever that she won't get into trouble.
11. There were so many people that they collected a lot of money.
12. There was so much snow that they could start the race.
13. We have so little money (= not enough) that we cannot buy the house.
14. The river had so much water that it could flood the whole valley.
15. The big countries have so many bombs that they could destroy the whole world several times.
16. There is so much time left that you can finish the exercises.
17. There were so few men that they could not put out the fire.
18. There is so much air in the tanks that we can dive down once more.
19. We have so little petrol left that we won't get to the next town.
20. There was so much room that we could park all the cars.
21. I'm so sleepy that I can't do my homework now.
22. Fred has so many skills that he will become a top player.
23. Many people are so poor that they can't buy food and clothes.
24. I have so many photos that I could fill three albums.
25. It was so cold that we did not go outside.
26. Don't worry, Max, there will be so much time tomorrow that you can finish your book.
27. Call a taxi, Joe! You are so drunk that you can't ride your bike.
28. There was so much wind that it made windsurfing dangerous.
29. On Christmas Eve the children were so excited that they could not sit still.
30. The new power station will produce so much energy that it will supply half the country.

PRESENT PARTICIPLE – Mittelwort der Gegenwart

- auch "1. Mittelwort" oder "Partizipium Präsens"
- eine *"ing-form"* ▶ *infinitive + ing* (Siehe auch "Gerund", Seite 28)
- kommt im Deutschen und im Englischen vor:

fließend	→	*flowing*
stehend	→	*standing*
spielend	→	*playing*

Present participle verwendest du in den folgenden Situationen:

(A) als Teil der ***progressive form*** ▶ ***form of "to be" + present participle***

*I **am taking** a shower.*
*Martha **is reading**.*
*They **were sleeping** when I came home.*

(B) nach bestimmten Verben ▶ ***verb + present participle***

*I **heard** you **quarrelling** with your sister again.*
*The boys **came running** up the hill.*
*We **watched** them **going** into the house.*

(C) zur Verkürzung oder Verknüpfung von Sätzen ▶

*Mum prepared breakfast **singing** a song.*
***Whistling** his favourite song, Joe left the house.*

(D) anstelle eines Gliedsatzes mit ***as, because, when*** oder ***while*** ▶

***Knowing** where Judy lived, I decided to visit her.*
(As I knew where Judy lived, I ...)

***Driving** through the country, we saw lots of churches.*
(While/As we were driving through the country, we ...)

(E) anstelle eines einschränkenden Relativsatzes ▶

*Guests **arriving** after 10 p.m. must call and say so.*
(Guests who arrive after 10 p.m. must ...)

*We noticed many strange birds **circling** above us.*
(... many strange birds that were circling above us.)

(F) als Adjektiv vor einem Nomen ▶ ***present participle + noun***

*Our room had no **running water**.*
*The **weeping willow** is a very pretty tree.*
*Never wake a **sleeping dog**.*

(A) PROGRESSIVE FORM / EXPANDED FORM

(Siehe dazu auch "Durchstarten Englisch – Dein Übungsbuch" für die 5. Klasse, Seite 86, für die 6. Klasse, Seite 84, und für die 7. Klasse, Seite 84 und 105, und in diesem Band ab Seite 23.)

present tense	*I*	***am***	***doing***	*my homework now.*
	He, She, It	***is***	***playing***	*in the garden.*
	We, You, They	***are***	***sitting***	*in the sun.*
past tense	*I*	***was***	***doing***	*working when you called.*
	He, She, It	***was***	***playing***	*in the garden at 5 o'clock.*
	We, You, They	***were***	***sitting***	*in the sun while I was asleep.*
future tense	*I, You, He, She …*	***will be***	***doing***	*something at this time on Friday.*
present perfect tense	*I*	***have been***	***doing***	*my homework for twenty minutes.*
	We, You, They	***have been***	***sitting***	*in the sun since this morning.*
	He, She, It	***has been***	***playing***	*in the garden for an hour.*
past perfect tense	*I, You, He, She …*	***had been***	***playing***	*for an hour when somebody called.*
future perfect tense	*I, You, He, She …*	***will be***	***playing***	*at 3 o'clock tomorrow afternoon.*

45 Fill in the correct tense of "progressive form".

Setze "progressive form" in der richtigen Zeitstufe ein.

1. Look, Sue (cry) .... ! Do you know what's the matter?
2. When I came home last night, the children (still, play) ....
3. Emily and Richard (live) .... in this house since 1968.
4. The man (lie) .... there for ten minutes before we noticed him.
5. Tomorrow at this time we (sit) .... on a train to Berlin.
6. You can't see Joe now. He (help) .... his dad in the garage.
7. The people (watch) .... while I (try) ....
   .... to put out the fire.
8. I (wait) .... for you for two hours. Where have you been?
9. What (you, do) .... since our last meeting?
10. Look at this weather! It (still, rain) .... – It's terrible, isn't it?
    It (rain) .... like this for four days now. When will it stop?

(B) VERB + PRESENT PARTICIPLE

(a) *see – watch – hear – feel – notice*

- Verben der (Sinnes-)Wahrnehmung ▶ vergleiche Kapitel *"Infinitive"*, Seite 47
- mit present participle eher bei nicht wiederholten, einzelnen Handlungen

  *I couldn't **hear you coming** home last night.* (▶ *last night = present participle)*
  *I can usually **hear you come** home late at night.* (▶ *usually = infinitive)*

(b) *go – come – keep – catch*

*The boys **go skiing** for a week every year.* ▶ ... gehen Schi fahren ...
*People **came rushing** out of the house.* ▶ ... kamen herausgelaufen ...
*They **kept playing** long into the night.* ▶ ... spielten weiter ...
*I **caught** Tom **kissing** my girlfriend.* ▶ ... erwischte ihn beim Küssen ...

46 Find the English verbs, fill in "present perfect" and translate the sentences into good German.
Finde die englischen Verben, setze "present participle" ein und übersetze die Sätze in gutes Deutsch.

1. Jackie is in her room, I think. Can't you hear her (*singen*) .... ?
2. From over there you can watch the planes (*abheben*) .... much better.
3. I could feel something (*krabbeln*) .... up my arm in the middle of the night.
4. Henry kept (*denken*) .... that he had made a mistake.
5. We saw you (*graben*) .... a hole in your garden. Are you looking for gold?
6. I can feel the air (*werden*) .... colder and colder. Winter is near.
7. After the match the players came (*laufen*) .... into the locker room.
8. One of my friends was caught (*fahren*) .... without a driving licence.
9. The car thief drove as fast as he could, but the police kept (*kommen*) .... closer and closer.
10. In summer we usually go (*schwimmen*) .... every week.
11. I can see you (*schauen*) .... out of the window every ten seconds. Are you expecting somebody?
12. The new pupil was caught (*stehlen*) .... money from his class mates.
13. When I looked out of the window, I saw Gina (*stehen*) .... there all alone.
14. The two hikers watched the clouds (*werden*) .... darker and darker.
15. The driver saw us (*stehen*) .... in the pouring rain, but he did not stop.
16. During the Maths test Mario was caught (*versuchen*) .... to cheat.
17. Mr. Myers says he saw us (*rauchen*) .... on the school grounds.
18. I could feel my problems (*anwachsen*) .... bigger and bigger.

19. When did you get in last night? I didn't hear you (*zusperren*) .... the door.
20. Yesterday at the supermarket I watched a woman (*geben*) .... some cosmetics into her coat pocket.
21. Yesterday I saw my new teacher (*gehen*) .... into a restaurant with a man.
22. From our hotel window we could see and hear the avalanche (*donnern*) .... down the mountainside.
23. My parents caught me (*schauen*) .... TV after midnight, which I mustn't do.
24. I noticed you (*sprechen*) .... with this man a minute ago. Who is he?
25. Jill was frightened when she saw the blood (*kommen*) .... from her nose.
26. After I had gone to bed, I could hear my dad (*schnarchen*) .... next door.
27. Iris could feel her headache (*werden*) .... better every hour.
28. I couldn't sleep because I could hear the rain (*klopfen*) .... on my window.
29. In spring Gerry goes (*fischen*) .... almost every day.
30. Every morning at ten to seven, old Mrs. Norris comes (*spazieren*) .... down the street with her poodle.
31. I hope you won't keep us (*warten*) .... so long again!
32. The men were caught (*versuchen*) .... to hide the stolen jewels.
33. I can smell something (*brennen*) .... ! Quick, let's have a look!
34. Don't keep me (*raten*) ...., please. Tell me what you know.
35. There is somebody in the room! I can hear him (*atmen*) .... !
36. Are you sure Joe is at home? – Yes, I've just heard him (*lachen*) ....
37. Do you often go (*schwimmen*) ...., Eric? – As often as I can.
38. Don't let me catch you (*klettern*) .... over my fence again!
39. When school is over, the children come (*laufen*) .... into the schoolyard.
40. Let's go back! I can feel the wind (*sich wandeln*) .... into a storm.
41. I've noticed you (*schauen*) .... at this picture. Do you like it?
42. I hope Farmer Jones doesn't catch us (*spielen*) .... war games on his land.
43. Where's the nearest phone box, please? – Well, keep (*folgen*) .... this street for about 300 yards. It's on your left, next to the supermarket.
44. This morning the headmaster saw us (*verlassen*) .... the school grounds.
45. We've watched you (*spielen*) .... with these kids. Do you know them?
46. I hope I will never catch you (*lügen*) .... to me because I hate liars!
47. At midnight, the vampires come (*kriechen*) .... out of their hiding places.
48. Did you notice anyone (*stehen*) .... around in the street yesterday?

(C) CONNECTING SENTENCES WITH PRESENT PARTICIPLE

- möglich **bei gleichzeitigen oder knapp aufeinanderfolgenden Handlungen**
- Bedingung: **gleiches Subjekt in beiden/allen Sätzen**
- "Haupthandlung" bleibt unverändert; "Nebenhandlung" wird durch *present participle* ausgedrückt

Mum prepared breakfast. She sang a song.

▶ *Mum prepared breakfast* ***singing*** *a song.* → "Frühstück" = Haupthandlung
→ "Singen" = Nebenhandlung

▶ ***Preparing*** *breakfast, Mum sang a song.* → "Frühstück" = Nebenhandlung
→ "Singen" = Haupthandlung

47 Connect or shorten the following sentences, using "present participle".

Verbinde oder verkürze die folgenden Sätze mit Hilfe von "present participle".
(2) ... zwei Möglichkeiten

1. Sally opened her wardrobe and showed me her new skirt. (2)
2. Dad took Mum by the arm and led her onto the dance floor. (2)
3. Our teacher stood near the board. She explained the homework. (2)
4. I ran through the garden and stumbled over a shovel.
5. My brother lay on the couch. He watched TV. (2)
6. Mum waved at our neighbours and went on mowing the lawn.
7. My sister looked up from her desk and saw a spider on the ceiling.
8. We all ate our ice creams and thought of Italy. (2)
9. Carol and Max came into the classroom. They laughed heartily. (2)
10. Patrick sat down at his desk and opened his books.
11. He put on his glasses and started to read the poem.
12. The actor rose from his seat and bowed in front of the audience.
13. The people clapped their hands. They welcomed the singer.
14. Manfred closed the door behind him. He threw the car key on the desk.
15. They put on their warm jackets and went out into the snow-covered garden.
16. Mum put aside the cutlery and finished her meal with a glass of red wine.
17. Grandpa lit his pipe and made himself comfortable on the couch. (2)
18. Aunt Dorothy had a cup of tea. She thought about the events of the last week. (2)
19. We drove through the countryside. We saw lots of rabbits rushing everywhere.
20. I read a book about South America. I fell asleep.
21. Ida combed her hair. She made up her mind to have it cut short.
22. Anna opened the book and came upon an old picture postcard from her grandfather.
23. Mum looked for her earrings in the living room and found Dad's watch under the sofa.
24. Dad put on his boots and left the house.
25. We took coffee on the balcony and watched the squirrels gathering nuts for the winter. (2)
26. While I was doing my homework, I had the idea of writing a letter to my aunt in Canada.

(D) INSTEAD OF A CLAUSE BEGINNING WITH "AS", "BECAUSE", "WHEN", "WHILE"

(anstelle eines Gliedsatzes, der mit *"as"*, *"because"*, *"when"* oder *"while"* beginnt)

- **Hauptsatz und Gliedsatz ("*clause*") müssen nicht dasselbe Subjekt haben**
- **Ausnahme:** Gliedsätze, die mit ***"while"*** **eingeleitet** werden

gleiches Subjekt → *"present participle"* am Satzbeginn

▶ *As **Joe** had no money left, **he** could not buy the CD.*
*__Joe__ could not buy the CD because **he** had no money left.*
*Having no money left, **Joe** could not buy the CD.*

▶ *While **you** were reading a book, **you** fell asleep.*
*Reading a book, **you** fell asleep.*

verschiedene Subjekte → *"present participle"* nach dem 1. Subjekt

▶ *When **the film** was over, **the people** went home.*
The film *being over,* **the people** *went home.*

▶ *As **the weather** had changed, **Julie** went swimming with her friends.*
***The weather** having changed, **Julie** went swimming with her friends.*

48 Replace the clauses with "present participles".

Ersetze die Gliedsätze durch "present participles".

1. While Sally and Dave were riding home from school, they saw a black cat.
   As the cat was hungry, he miaowed loudly.
   As the children had no pet, they took the cat home with them.
   They offered the cat some milk because they had no other food at home.
   As the little cat was tired, it went to sleep at once.
   When the kids looked at the sleeping cat, they felt they had done the right thing.
2. When Verena walks to school, she usually meets Lena and Carmen.
3. As the boys had only 2 £, they bought some potato chips and mineral water.
4. As Dave was all alone, he decided to ring up Sally.
5. As Mum was ill, Dad and I had to do the cooking.
6. When I was riding my scooter down the street, I was stopped by the police.
7. As I had no school yesterday, I decided to stay in bed till ten.
8. While I was talking to my teacher, I had a crazy idea.
9. As the bus was late, we missed the beginning of the film.
10. When Mum walked through the empty house last night, she heard strange noises.
11. As petrol is so expensive today, many people travel by train again.
12. As Joe wants to buy a new PC, he is saving all his money.

13. While the boys were watching TV, they ate everything that was in the fridge.
14. As the crowd was out of control, the police decided to use tear gas.
15. When the old lady left the shop, she carried a heavy bag.
16. When Dave went out to play with his friends, he forgot to switch off the lights.
17. As we had just eaten lunch at school, we were not hungry at all.
18. As Eric was a rich man, we asked him for some money.
19. When winter was over, the bears woke up from their sleep.
20. As Dad came back to his car, he noticed that it had a flat tyre.
21. We decided to have dinner indoors because the evening grew colder and colder.
22. As the dog was very thirsty, it drank a bowl full of water.
23. As my dad is an expert on computers, people often ask him for advice.
24. While the Queen was riding along the boulevard, she waved at the spectators.
25. As the boys did not know the answer, they sat still and looked embarrassed.
26. When the diver came back to the surface, he showed us the pearl that he had found.
27. As the summer was so hot, Mum bought herself a straw hat.
28. Dennis does all kinds of jobs because he needs the money badly.
29. When Steffi felt that she would lose the match, she stopped playing.
30. When dinner was ready, Mum called us into the dining room.
31. Martin tried to cross the lake because he was a good swimmer.
32. Sally hurt her knee when she fell down the ladder.
33. As the weather was perfect, we decided to have a picnic.
34. As the night was cold, we closed all the windows.
35. As time passed by so slowly, we decided to take a walk around the block.
36. As my friend Ken always plays the fool, I don't want to go out with him any more.
37. Paul can plant what he wants because he is the owner of the garden.
38. When Dad drives home from work, he listens to classical music.
39. When winter was over, Mum put our boots away.
40. As Max is a good skier, we don't worry when he goes down steep slopes.
41. We did not speak about the new bike with Dad because he was tired from work.
42. Sue walked home quickly because she felt a headache coming.
43. As the horses were hungry, Jason went out to feed them.
44. As Sunday was coming nearer, Mum was getting nervous because she still didn't know what to cook.
45. They asked Brian to play for the school team because he was the best player.
46. As I was hungry, I had a cup of tea and some biscuits.
47. We felt bored because we had nothing to do.
48. When Dad reads a good book, he forgets the world around him.
49. When the boys had left the classroom, the girls could speak freely.
50. When the clock struck midnight, the ghosts came out of their hiding places.
51. As the windows were open all night, the air in the room was cool and fresh.
52. We had to clean the pots and pans ourselves because the dishwasher was out of order.
53. As the headmistress was waiting for us, we hurried to meet her in time.
54. When our neighbours returned from their weekend trip, they found the garage door open.
55. As our car was new and fast, we knew we could get there in less than an hour.
56. We carried Simon down the stairs because he was too week to walk.

(E) INSTEAD OF A RELATIVE CLAUSE

▶ *The people <u>who live</u> in the Arctic region are called Inuit.*
*The people **living** in the Arctic region are called Inuit.*

▶ *In Scotland we saw lots of sheep <u>that were grazing</u> in the Highlands.*
*In Scotland we saw lots of sheep **grazing** in the Highlands.*

▶ *I know all the flowers <u>which grow</u> in my garden.*
*I know all the flowers **growing** in my garden.*

Bedingung: einschränkender Relativsatz (*defining relative clause*)
keine Kommas

In einem Satz können auch **mehrere *present participles*** vorkommen:

▶ *<u>When I came</u> home from school, I **saw** a man <u>who was standing</u> opposite our house.*
***Coming** home from school, I **saw** a man **standing** opposite our house.*
Haupthandlung = unverändert

49 Use "present participles" wherever you can.

Verwende "present participles", wo immer es geht.

<u>example:</u> When we left school, we saw a woman who was talking to herself. ▶
Leaving school, we saw a woman *talking* to herself.

1. When Mum was walking through the park, she noticed an old woman who was sleeping on a bench.
2. As Peter opened the bag, he found chewing gum that was sticking to one side.
3. All the trees that stand in the way of the planned landing strip will be cut down.
4. When Joe left the restaurant, he noticed a little boy who was trying to cross the street.
5. Yvonne found a letter that was lying on the floor when she opened the door to her flat.
6. As I am Mary's best friend, I gave her the picture that is hanging on the wall of her room now.
7. When Robert the Bruce was resting in a lonely hut, he watched a spider that was trying to swing from one rafter to the other.
8. As I looked out of the window, I saw a dog that was running around nervously.
9. When Mr. Winters opened the door to the classroom, he found a poster that was stuck to the board.
10. As I wanted to surprise Joe, I bought him the DVD that is lying on the cupboard.
11. When the school year was over, my parents bought me the bike that is standing over there.
12. As I was watching the news on TV tonight, I saw a woman who wore the same coat as my aunt.
13. As I am very keen on sweets, I ate three chocolate bars.
14. Icicles that fall from roofs can be very dangerous.
15. The two girls who are waiting for me at the entrance are my cousins.
16. As mum was tidying the kitchen, she found a ring that was lying under the table.
17. As Joe had finished first in his class, he found a job with a company that produces mobile phones.
18. While Gemma was waiting for her bus, she noticed a stranger who was taking pictures of her.

50 Use present participles in every sentence (sometimes one, sometimes more).

Verwende "present participles" in jedem Satz (manchmal nur eines, manchmal mehrere).

1. When I came into the room, I heard Mum. She was singing "Maria" from West Side Story.
2. As we were driving through the country, we saw many cows. They were grazing in the meadows.
3. When I'm playing computer games, I forget all the problems around me.
4. When we watched the video, we remembered the sights of London.
5. As Dad knew Mr. McCullough, he was sent to talk to him.
6. Our team played superbly for ninety minutes and won the match.
7. When Dave was hopping down the stairs, he fell and hurt his knees.
8. My sister stood outside the disco and wondered if she should go in.
9. We stood in the middle of the room and looked at the beautiful furniture.
10. The car drove into a group of cyclists and knocked three of them over.
11. I found Dad in his office. He was studying some papers.
12. As Romina did not know what to say, she said nothing.
13. While Dad was preparing breakfast, he cut his finger.
14. While Mum was swimming in the sea, she lost her favourite earring.
15. While we were walking along the pond, we saw a snake that was eating a frog.
16. When I looked into my sister's room, I saw her sitting on the floor. She was writing her diary.
17. My sister came into my room. She asked me for some money.
18. The young man who was talking to the women on the tram was a pickpocket.
19. I opened my wallet. I noticed that I had forgotten my money.
20. As we drove to town last night, we got stuck in the traffic jam.
21. Sally entered the room and said hello to everybody.
22. Our maths teacher walked from pupil to pupil during the exam. He tried to help them.
23. Tom tried to cool himself. He jumped into the pool.
24. Dr. Lecter was walking home after work. He was thinking about his patients.
25. As Mum thought she was alone, she walked around in her underwear.
26. When I looked into my sister's room, I saw how she kissed a boy.
27. During an exam, the teacher sits behind a desk and takes notes.
28. In summer, I often watch the butterflies in the garden. They are flying from flower to flower.
29. We tried to find a decent hotel. We drove around for hours.
30. When Frank looked at the book for the first time, he realised that it was absolute rubbish.
31. Granny sat in her rocking chair all day long. She looked at old photographs and newspaper clips.
32. As George is an engineer, he has to know a lot about maths.
33. My sister came into my room. She asked me to help her with her computer.
34. As Florian is the cleverest boy in my class, he is well liked by the teachers.
35. The boys followed Ralph's orders because he was the leader of the group.
36. Jill woke up and saw a mouse in her room.
37. Frodo noticed an ugly creature that followed them everywhere.
38. We watched the circus people. They set up the big tent in the big car park.
39. As Marion works outdoors most of the time, she has got a nice suntan.
40. The President of the USA has a very hard job because he is the most powerful person in the world.
41. As you have done forty sentences, you can take a rest now.

"ING-FORM" OR INFINITIVE? – "ing-Form" oder Infinitiv?

- Verben, die **zwingend den Infinitiv / die Nennform** verlangen:

  ▶ *modal verbs, let, make, decide, hope, promise …* → siehe ab Seite 43

- Verben, die **zwingend eine "ing-Form" verlangen (*gerund*** oder ***present participle*):**

  ▶ *avoid, consider, imagine, look forward to, cannot help …* → siehe ab Seite 30
  ▶ *go, come, keep, catch …* → siehe ab Seite 64

- Verben, die **entweder mit dem Infinitiv oder mit dem Gerund** auftreten:

(a) gleiche Bedeutung:

▶ ***begin – start – continue***
It started to rain = started raining while I was walking home..
Our team continued to win = continued winning after the first match.
After the speeches were over, the choir began to sing = began singing.

▶ ***like – love – prefer – hate***
Dad likes to surprise = surprising us with small gifts.
I really love to speak = speaking with you.
Maggie prefers to buy = buying her shoes in Italy.
Jenny hates to leave = leaving the party so early.

▶ **aber: *would (like/love/prefer/hate)* nur mit Infinitiv**
I would like to read this story. → Ich möchte diese Geschichte lesen.
(*I like to read/reading.* → Ich lese gern.)

(b) geringer Bedeutungsunterschied: *verb + infinitive* ≈ *verb + "ing-form"*

▶ ***verb + infinitive*** (siehe auch S. 47): meist für die gesamte Handlung; eher allgemein gehalten; keine bestimmte Handlung
I always see them come home late at night.
We've never heard you complain.

▶ ***verb + "ing-form"*** (siehe auch S. 64): meist für eine bestimmte Handlung; geschah/geschieht zu einer bestimmten Zeit
Let's stand over there where we can watch them playing.
I want to go inside. I feel the air getting colder and colder.

(c) großer Bedeutungsunterschied: *verb + infinitive* ≠ *verb + "ing-form"*

	verb + infinitive	*verb + "ing-form"*
▶ *forget*	*Joe **forgot to ask** his parents.* (... vergaß, sie zu fragen.) → hätte er tun sollen = notwendige Handlung	*He **forgot asking** them.* (... vergaß, dass er sie gefragt hat.) → hat er schon getan = bereits geschehen
▶ *need*	*We **need to mow** the lawn.* (Wir müssen den Rasen mähen.) → Notwendigkeit, Zwang (aktiv) = wir müssen etwas tun	*The lawn **needs mowing**.* (Der Rasen muss gemäht werden.) → Notwendigkeit, Zwang (passiv) = etwas muss getan werden
▶ *remember*	***Remember to be** on time.* (Denke daran, pünktlich zu sein.) notwendige Handlung = Vergiss nicht, ...!	*I **remember being** on time.* (Ich erinnere mich, dass ich pünktlich war.) Erinnerung an Vergangenes = ich kann mich daran erinnern
▶ *stop*	*He **stopped to speak** with me.* (Er blieb stehen, um mit mir zu sprechen.) unterbrochene Handlung, um etwas anderes zu tun	*He **stopped speaking** with me.* (Er hörte auf, mit mir zu sprechen.) abgebrochene/beendete Handlung
▶ *try*	*We **tried to pay** with euros.* (Wir versuchten ... zu bezahlen.) konkreter Versuch, etwas zu tun = wir versuch(t)en es	***Try paying** with dollars!* (Versuche, mit ... zu bezahlen!) Vorschlag, etwas zu tun = versuche es doch

51 Infinitive or "ing-form"? Cross out the wrong word.

Infinitiv oder "ing-Form"? Streiche das falsche Wort durch.

1. I *tried to call / tried calling* you four times yesterday, but you weren't in.
2. The garden fence *needs to paint / needs painting.*
3. *Remember to answer / Remember answering* Frank's email. It's important.
4. On the way to work Dad *stopped to post / stopped posting* a letter.
5. Joe will never *forget to crash / forget crashing* into the tree.
6. If you can't turn the key, *try to put / try putting* a drop of oil on it.
7. I'm sorry I *forgot to do / forgot doing* the dishes, Mum. I'll do them in a minute.
8. You *need to study / need studying* harder before the next exam.
9. Do you *remember to show / remember showing* us the plan? Could we see it again, please?
10. How many times have you *stopped to smoke / stopped smoking*? – Five or six times, but it was no good. I can't give it up.
11. Look at those flowers! They *need to water / need watering* badly.
12. Grandpa *tried to remember / tried remembering* where he had put his pipe, but it was no good.
13. Annie did not *stop to think / stop thinking* if her plan was good or not; she just went ahead.
14. I *remember to buy / remember buying* this sweater in California.
15. If you need help with the history project, *try to get / try getting* the new Blu-ray on "Ancient Rome".

52 Infinitive or "ing-form"? Find the correct form of the verb.

Infinitiv oder "ing-Form"? Finde die richtige Form des Verbs.

1. Fred, have you finished (read) .... ?
2. We'd like (open) .... the presents now.
3. Nick prefers (wear) .... jeans and trainers.
4. On Sunday I watched my sisters (play) .... hockey.
5. Linda managed (put) .... all her books onto the shelf.
6. I'm angry, because Nina has refused (come) .... my party again.
7. My dad loves (ride) .... his motorbike.
8. After an hour the boys continued (play) ....
9. Last year, Tim stopped (smoke) ....
   He had tried (give up) .... (smoke) ....
   three times before, but he never really succeeded in (do) .... so.
   This time he had (stop) .... because he had asthma.
   If he had continued (smoke) .... , he would have risked (get)
   .... seriously ill.
   A friend had said to him, "Why don't you try (eat) .... sugar-free sweets
   instead of (smoke) .... ?"
   And really, so far he has managed (keep) .... away from cigarettes.
10. Dad stopped a passer-by (ask) .... him for the way.
11. I'd love (fly) .... a helicopter one day.
    I love (do) .... exciting things.
12. Mum and Dad are here. I can hear them (talk) ....
13. "(eat) .... sweets is dangerous for your teeth", the dentist said.
    But it's very difficult (give up) .... something one likes so much.
14. I remember (read) .... this book last year, and I did not really enjoy
    (do) .... so!
15. Look, somebody has forgotten (lock) .... the door again. I hate (come)
    .... home and (find) .... the door open.
    Imagine someone (walk) .... into the house and (steal)
    .... something.
16. I'm sure I didn't forget (lock) .... it. I clearly remember (check)
    .... all the doors and windows before we left.
17. Have you ever watched Bill (do) .... his card tricks? They are amazing.

18. Jack hates (sing) .... and he hates (dance) ....
Why doesn't he try (talk) .... to Betty about it? Perhaps she will stop (ask) .... him (go) .... to the disco.

19. Nelly has caught a cold although we tried (make) .... her (wear) .... a warmer jacket. However, as usual, he refused (listen) .... to us.

20. I thought you loved (take) .... walks in the rain. – No, I don't! I hate (get) .... wet. I much prefer (stay) .... inside when it's pouring.

21. The walls of my room need (paint) .... I think I'll try (paint) .... them blue and green this time because I like (try out) .... new colours.

22. Today we go to the supermarket (buy) .... our food. We are not used to (hunt) .... and (fish) .... any more.

23. Digital watches are very comfortable. They don't need (wind) .... up!

24. Please stop (make) .... such a noise, children! I am trying (finish) .... my homework.

25. Sally can't help (cough) .... I think she's caught a cold from (play) .... in the garden.

26. Would you mind (open) .... the window? I don't like (work) .... in a room with stuffy air.

27. Your glasses need (clean) .... Would you like me (do) .... it for you?

28. What's wrong with Mike? He avoids (speak) .... with me.

29. Go on (work) .... , boys. It's late and your mother doesn't like (wait) ....

30. Tom made us all very angry by (go) .... away without (say) .... a word.

31. I don't like people (smoke) .... in my living room. – Well, I don't like people (smoke) .... at all.

32. Daniel is fun. I couldn't help (laugh) .... about his jokes.

33. Kids usually like (play) .... games, but most of them dislike (work) .... for school.

34. I've always been told (not talk) .... to strangers.

53 Infinitive or "ing-form"? Find the correct form of the verb.

Infinitiv oder "ing-Form"? Finde die richtige Form des Verbs.

1. After an hour we began (understand) .... what they wanted to tell us.
2. Would you mind (show) .... me your new car? – No, I'd love to.
3. Danny made up his mind (disguise) .... himself for the party by (dress) .... up as a girl.
4. (smoke) .... during meals is a very bad habit.
5. Dad tried (explain) .... the dangers, but my friends and I refused (listen) .... to him.
6. Cindy is so stupid! I can't stand (listen) .... to her any more.
7. Don't forget (put) .... out the light in the living room and the hall before (go) .... to bed.
8. It's no use (wait) .... for these people any more. They won't (come) .... anyway.
9. Sally, I'm really looking forward to (see) .... you in the holidays.
10. John really dislikes (be) .... the centre of the party.
11. Dave kept (ask) .... his mother for money, but she refused (give) .... him more.
12. Do you remember (give) .... Sheila your new email address ?
13. In fairy tales, little girls are afraid of (meet) .... the big bad wolf. And in real life, they wouldn't like (have) .... a wolf as a pet, either.
14. I know my hair needs (cut) ...., but I don't seem (have) .... the time to do it.
15. There is little use (buy) .... a sports car if you live in a city.
16. After (talk) .... about the problem for over an hour, we broke up without (reach) .... a sensible decision.
17. At the beginning we enjoyed (listen) .... to the men, but then we got tired of (hear) .... the same jokes again and again.
18. I tried (forget) .... Justin, but I couldn't. All my friends said he wasn't worth (think) .... about, but I disagree.
19. What a life! Imagine (get) .... up at five in the morning every day!
20. Look at Jean! She seems (be) .... ill. – Yes, she says she can feel her headache (get) .... stronger.
21. The doctor told us (see) .... him again in six months.

22. After (read) .... the menu we decided (not enter) .... the restaurant.
23. The dog did not really want (do) .... what I was telling it.
24. I'd love (have) .... the chance of (see) .... you again soon.
25. Ben hates (get) .... up early and (wash) .... with cold water, so he decided (stay) .... in bed a little longer.
26. I couldn't help (ask) .... Bill why he didn't like me any more. I had the feeling that he was trying (avoid) .... (meet) .... me again after the party.
27. As the concert came nearer and nearer, Vincent decided (take) .... a few piano lessons with an expert.
28. The new doctor did not let the children (play) .... outside.
29. Can you imagine (live) .... in such a house? – No, I would begin (feel) .... uneasy.
30. The man was caught (try) .... (sell) .... stolen goods.
31. I don't understand why Brenda wants (marry) .... Kevin.
32. Has anybody mentioned (find) .... the stolen pictures?
33. Look at Joe! He's busy (flirt) .... with Helen, so it's not use (try) .... (speak) .... with him now.
34. Psychologists say that babies can (swim) .... before they start (walk) ....
35. Grandma asked us (stop) .... (make) .... such a noise.
36. Would you mind (take) .... this letter to the post office, please?
37. I'm really fond of (watch) .... horror films, but I'm not interested in (read) .... horror stories.
38. Mellie likes boys, but she hates (wait) .... for them.
39. Dad finally gave up (smoke) ...., but now he wants (have) .... a piece of chocolate after each meal.
40. Everybody wants (live) .... a long life, but nobody likes (get) .... old.
41. Sometimes it is quite difficult (spell) .... English words correctly.

54 Infinitive or "ing-form"? Translate into good English.

Infinitiv oder "ing-Form"? Übersetze in gutes Englisch.

1. Wir sollten lieber zuhause bleiben.
2. Sandy bat mich, ihn zum Bahnhof zu bringen.
3. Ich freue mich schon darauf, mit Nicole auszugehen.
4. Es macht mir nichts aus, mit dem Rad zu fahren.
5. Unsere Freunde erlaubten uns, ihr Swimmingpool zu benutzen.
6. Möchtest du, dass ich gehe oder bleibe?
7. Ich kann es nicht ertragen, ein Tier leiden zu sehen.
8. Fred erinnert sich, dass er mit mir über den Film gesprochen hat.
9. Wir dürfen nicht vergessen, Henry anzurufen.
10. Es hat keinen Sinn, mit dem Mann zu sprechen.
11. Man erwartet, dass wir pünktlich kommen.
12. Ich wünsche mir, dass die Buben mit uns zusammen arbeiten.
13. Wir würden lieber ins Kino gehen.
14. Gina ist es gewöhnt, spät schlafen zu gehen.
15. Sie blieben stehen, um nach dem Weg zu fragen.
16. Großvater hörte mit 80 auf zu fahren.
17. Mutter lässt mich mein Zimmer immer allein aufräumen.
18. New York ist eine sehenswerte Stadt.
19. Ich sah jemand aus dem Haus laufen.
20. Hast du mich gestern nachhause kommen gehört?
21. Amelie hofft, ihre amerikanische Freundin bald zu besuchen.
22. Wir habe keine Ahnung, was wir tun sollen.
23. Martha hätte es gern, wenn wir früher kämen.
24. Joes Vater lässt ihn manchmal mit dem Auto fahren.
25. Mr. Lafitte sagte, wir sollten einen Aufsatz über Vulkane schreiben.
26. Großmutter will nicht, dass wir die Rechnung bezahlen.
27. Ich möchte dir raten, deine Eltern zu informieren.
28. Erwartest du, dass Tina dich anruft?
29. Hör nicht auf! Lies weiter!
30. Wir sind damit beschäftigt, Möbelkataloge durchzublättern.
31. Norma fuhr mit dem Taxi, statt auf den Bus zu warten.
32. Da der Bus Verspätung hatte, gingen wir zu Fuß.
33. Oma bäckt gerne Kuchen.
34. Ich gebe zu, dass ich einen Fehler gemacht habe.
35. Soll ich dir helfen? (= Möchtest du, dass ...?)
36. Wir würden gerne mit euch tanzen.
37. Hör auf, mich anzustarren!
38. Bill ist ziemlich gut im Imitieren von Vogelstimmen.
39. Man sagt, Joggen ist sehr gesund.
40. Mir ist heute nicht nach Kinogehen zumute.
41. Ich schlage vor, wir beenden diese Übung jetzt.

PHRASAL VERBS

verb + preposition mit unterschiedlicher Bedeutung zum ursprünglichen Verb, zB

go	→	gehen, fahren	▶	*go on*	→	weitermachen, fortsetzen
look	→	schauen	▶	*look for*	→	suchen
put	→	stellen, setzen legen, geben	▶	*put off*	→	verschieben

A	
act out	aufführen
ask out	zum Ausgehen einladen
B	
bring about	verursachen, herbeiführen
C	
call off	absagen
calm down	sich beruhigen
care for	sich um jemand kümmern; (etwas oder jemand) mögen
carry on	weitermachen,
carry out	durchführen, umsetzen
catch up	einholen, aufschließen
check in	einchecken, Gepäck abfertigen
come across	zufällig auf etwas stoßen, zufällig jemand begegnen
come along	mitkommen
E	
eat up	aufessen
eat out	auswärts essen, essen gehen
F	
fill in	einsetzen, ausfüllen
fill up	volltanken
find out	herausfinden, dahinterkommen
G	
get along	mit jemand auskommen
get in/on	einsteigen
get off	aussteigen
get on with	mit jemand auskommen; mit etwas fortfahren
get over	mit etwas fertig werden; über etwas hinwegkommen
get up	(vom Liegen) aufstehen
go on	weitermachen, fortsetzen
grow up	erwachsen werden
H	
hand in	(Hefte, Arbeiten) abgeben
hand out	aushändigen, überreichen

hang out	(mit Freunden) herumhängen
hang up	den Telefonhörer auflegen
hear from	Nachricht von jemand erhalten
hear of	von etwas oder jemand hören
K	
keep on	(Gewand) anbehalten
L	
let down	im Stich lassen
lie down	hinlegen, niederlegen
look after	auf etwas/jemand aufpassen
look down on	auf jemand herabsehen
look for	suchen
look forward to	sich auf etwas freuen
look into	(eine Sache) untersuchen
look on	zuschauen
look out	aufpassen, Acht geben
look up to	zu jemand aufschauen
M	
make up	(eine Geschichte) erfinden; sich schminken
N	
name after	nach jemand benennen
P	
pay back	zurückzahlen, heimzahlen
pick up	aufheben; jemand abholen
put off	(auf später) verschieben
put on	anziehen
put out	(Feuer) löschen
R	
ring up	anrufen
run into	zufällig jemand treffen
run out of	etwas nicht mehr haben
S	
show up	erscheinen, "auftauchen"
slow down	langsamer werden, bremsen
stay over	über Nacht bleiben

T	
take back	zurücknehmen
take off	(Kleider) ausziehen, abnehmen; (Flugzeug) starten
talk back to	zurückreden
tear down	abreißen, niederreißen
tear up	zerreißen, in Stücke reißen
try on	(Gewand) anprobieren
try out	erproben, prüfen, testen
turn away	sich abwenden; jemand abweisen/wegschicken
turn around	umdrehen, wenden
turn down	(Radio) leiser drehen; (Bitte, Angebot) ablehnen

turn into	sich in (etwas) verwandeln
turn on/off	ein-/ausschalten
turn out	sich erweisen, herausstellen
turn up	(Radio) lauter stellen; erscheinen, "auftauchen"
W	
wake up	aufwachen, munter werden; jemand wecken
watch out	aufpassen, Acht geben
wind up	(Uhr) aufziehen
work out	ausarbeiten, erarbeiten; (Sport) trainieren
write down	auf-/niederschreiben, notieren

55 Fill in the suitable phrasal verb.

Setze das passende "phrasal verb" ein.

1. We are going to (*aufführen*) .... some scenes from "Grease" in class.
2. I'd like to (*zum Ausgehen einladen*) .... Monica ...., but I don't know how.
3. The new headmaster (*führte herbei*) .... big changes in our school.
4. They had to (*absagen*) .... the match because of the bad weather.
5. I was so angry at Joe! It took me a long time to (*mich beruhigen*) ....
6. Dad doesn't (*mögen*) .... coffee. He likes tea better.
7. Who (*sich kümmern um*) .... your pets when you are away?
8. Please (*macht weiter*) .... ! Don't let me stop you!
9. A soldier has to (*ausführen*) .... the orders of his officers.
10. We'll have to hurry if we want to (*einholen*) .... Ginger and Fred.
11. Before you (*einchecken*) .... your luggage, put a name tag on it.
12. While I was reading the newspaper, I (*zufällig auf etwas stoßen*) ....
    an article about our garden party at school.
13. I was at this garden party because my friends had asked me to (*mitkommen*) ....
14. If you want dessert, you must first (*aufessen*) .... the spinach!
15. We all like (*auswärts essen*) .... We prefer Chinese or Greek cooking.
16. The headline said, "Please (*einsetzen*) .... all necessary information!"
17. (*Voll tanken*) .... the car with regular petrol, please.
18. When did you (*herausfinden*) .... that you had won the competition?
19. It's not easy to (*auskommen*) .... with Marcia. She can be difficult!

20. Hurry up and (*einsteigen*) .... the car! We must go!
21. Where must I (*aussteigen*) .... for the museum? – It's the first stop.
22. Mary still hasn't (*hinwegkommen*) .... her fight with Peter.
23. During the school year I (*aufstehen*) .... at 6.30 in the morning.
24. Let's not stop now! Let's (*weitermachen*) .... for another hour or so.
25. Bill is 21, but he's still such a child. When will he (*erwachsen werden*) ....?
26. We have to (*abgeben*) .... our essays next Monday.
27. Tom, can you please (*austeilen*) .... the test books?
28. At the weekends, I like (*herumhängen*) .... with my friends.
29. When Jack calls again, I'm going to (*den Hörer auflegen*) .... at once!
30. Have you (*von ... hören*) .... Lynn again? – Yes, she's sent an email.
31. Angkor? What's Angkor? I've never (*davon gehört*) .... it.
32. You can (*anbehalten*) .... your shoes if you want to.
33. I don't like Joe any more. He's (*im Stich lassen*) .... me .... so often!
34. If you're tired, you can (*hinlegen*) .... on the sofa for a while.
35. Helen, can you please (*aufpassen*) .... my cat while I'm gone?
36. I hate teachers who (*herabschauen*) .... on their students.
37. Mum, where's my sweater? – I don't know. Go and (*suchen*) .... it!
38. Kate is sweet! I'm (*freuen*) .... going out with her again.
39. Police are (*untersuchen*) .... the burglaries in our street.
40. Lots of people (*schauten zu*) .... but nobody helped.
41. (*Pass auf*) ....! There's a car coming!
42. Our Maths teacher is great. We all (*zu ihm aufschauen*) ....
43. Bob's stories about how good he is are not true. He just (*erfindet*) .... them ....
44. The Rockefeller Center in New York is (*benannt nach*) .... John D. Rockefeller, Junior.
45. I hate Philip! One day I will (*heimzahlen*) .... him .... for what he did to me.
46. My train arrives at 4.15. Can you (*abholen*) .... me .... at the station, please?
47. Come on, Eric, do it now! You always (*verschieben*) .... everything.
48. (*Zieh an*) .... your shoes and let's go! We're late!
49. After half an hour, the firemen managed to (*löschen*) .... the fire.
50. I can't speak with you now, but I'll (*anrufen*) .... you .... later today.
51. When we were in the shopping centre yesterday, we (*trafen zufällig*) .... Joe and his friends.

52. Our neighbours returned early from their holidays because they had (*nicht mehr haben*) .... money.

53. We waited for two hours, but Kevin didn't (*erscheinen*) ....

54. Please (*langsamer fahren*) ...., Dad. I'm afraid if you drive so fast.

55. Mum, can Jeannie (*über Nacht bleiben*) ...., please?

56. The PC didn't work, but they didn't want to (*zurücknehmen*) .... it ....

57. What I like best about flying is when the plane (*abheben*) ....

58. You have to (*ausziehen*) .... your shoes before you enter their house.

60. Have you heard? They are going to (*niederreißen*) .... the old church.

61. Colin was so angry that he (*zerreißen*) .... Melanie's letter.

62. I like these shoes! Can I (*anprobieren*) .... them .... ?

63. Dad is going to buy a new motorbike, but he wants to (*testen*) .... it .... before he buys it.

64. The girl was asking for help, but the people just (*sich abwenden*) ....

65. Dad missed the right road, so we had to (*umdrehen*) .... and go back.

66. Children, can you please (*leiser drehen*) .... the radio? I'm studying.

67. I really wanted to help Julia with her maths problems, but she (*zurückweisen*) .... my offer. I guess she's still mad at me.

68. Count Dracula (*verwandelte sich*) .... a giant bat and flew away.

69. (*Schalte ein*) .... the TV or (*schalte aus*) .... it ...., but don't play around with it!

70. At first, we didn't believe Rudy, but then it (*stellte sich heraus*) .... that he had been right with everything he had said.

71. More than forty people (*tauchten auf*) .... at Jim's concert.

72. I (*wachte auf*) .... because I had heard strange noises in my dream.

73. (*Pass auf*) .... ! The lights are changing to red!

74. The old clock has stopped. Did you forget to (*aufziehen*) .... it .... ?

75. It took scientists many years to (*ausarbeiten*) .... the laws of nature.

76. The detective (*schrieb auf*) .... every word the witness said.

77. Grandma used to say, "(*iss auf*) .... or the sun won't shine tomorrow."

78. (*Beruhige dich*) ...., Julia! I'm sure there is no reason to worry.

79. Steven is really nice. He (*auskommen*) .... with everyone.

80. When I (*erwachsen werden*) ...., I want to be a web designer.

81. Where did you get this brochure, boys? – A man (*teilte sie aus*) .... in town.

PREPOSITIONS – Vorwörter

Wichtigste Aufgabe von Präpositionen ▶ Beziehung zwischen einem Verb und einem anderen Satzteil herstellen

räumliche Beziehung ▶ ***prepositions of place:*** *under, over, in, through …*

zeitliche Beziehung ▶ ***prepositions of time:*** *from … to, since, till, after …*

andere Beziehungen ▶ ***other prepositions:*** *with, in spite of …*

Manche Präpositionen werden sowohl räumlich als auch zeitlich oder in anderer Bedeutung verwendet, zum Beispiel *"**in**"*.

place → *Joe is **in** the room.*
time → *Joe was born **in** 1993.*
"other" → *Joe will keep the date **in** mind.*

56 Fill in suitable prepositions of place. Choose from the box.

Setze passende "prepositions of place" (Vorwörter des Ortes) ein. Wähle von der "box" aus.

above – across – at – away – behind – below – beside – between – in – in front of – from – from … to – next to – on – opposite – over – out of – through – to – under

1. The woman with the big hat was sitting exactly .... me, so I couldn't see anything.
2. After school we often meet .... the corner of Parsons Street and South Avenue.
3. Sally threw her ball .... our kitchen window. Luckily it was open, so it didn't break.
4. Forty years ago Grandpa planted a chestnut tree .... our garden.
5. Our neighbour went straight .... my mum to tell her the news.
6. Our dog chased the neighbour's cat .... the garden.
7. From the top of the tree Danny could see the people far .... him.
8. Last year Carmen sat .... Lena and Jasmine in class 3b.
9. Our house has two floors. We live on the ground floor, and the Millers live .... us.
10. Dad and I could see a helicopter flying high .... us.
11. The River Danube flows .... many European countries.
12. Can you count .... one .... ten in Danish?
13. Every weekend my friends and I go .... the cinema or .... the disco.
14. Grandma's little dog usually sleeps .... her bed.
15. Two men came .... the house and got .... their car.
16. The letter "D" comes .... "C" and "E".
17. My sister's desk is .... mine, so I can always see her face.
18. In our car, I sit .... the driver in the first row because I usually read the map.
19. The old woman tried to walk .... the road, but the cars did not stop.

20. Look, there are Laura and Mike. I think they are coming .... the sports club.

21. Every day three or four jets fly .... our town. That's not too much noise.

22. Ken, why are you hiding .... the door? I know where you are!

23. Melvin was running right .... me when he stumbled and fell.

24. Please put the books .... the shelf, if you find enough room.

25. Human beings cannot breathe .... water without air tanks.

26. Our plane took .... from an airstrip in the middle of nowhere.

27. The bottle fell .... the floor and broke apart.

28. When the film was over, my friends came .... the cinema.

29. Stand up, George! You are sitting .... my chair again!

30. Melons grow .... the ground, peanuts grow .... it.

31. If you stand .... the board, nobody can read what you have written.

32. Hurry up, Ben! We're waiting for you .... the corner.

33. Get .... my bike at once! I didn't say you could use it, did I?

34. The shed stands .... one of the corners of the garden.

35. The New York marathon leads .... all five districts of the city.

36. It's very hot today, isn't it? – Oh yes. It must be .... 30 degrees.

37. This road leads .... the mountains, from Austria to Italy.

38. Have you seen my briefcase? – Yes, Dad. It's .... your desk, where it always is. (2)

39. On the school bus I usually sit .... Judy. This way it's easier to talk.

40. I live at number 6, Main Street, and Sue lives at number 7. That's directly .... the street. Her house is .... my house.

41. Is Gloria .... her room? – No, she isn't. She has gone .... town.

42. Next summer we'll visit Uncle Max .... Australia. I hope he will go .... Bondi Beach with us.

43. Pierluigi comes .... Italy, but his English is fantastic.

44. We sat down .... the trees because it was cooler there.

45. Dad often watches the stars .... with his telescope.

46. The train journey to Britain took us .... two countries, Germany and Belgium.

47. If you want to know where I've hidden your love letters, look .... the books .... your desk.

48. Valentina ran .... the house and locked the door .... her.

49. Then Danny fell .... the tree and landed .... the grass.

57 Fill in suitable prepositions of time. Choose from the box.

Setze passende "prepositions of time" (Vorwörter der Zeit) ein. Wähle von der "box" aus.

after – at – before – by – for – from ... to – in – on – since – until

1. Our new neighbours said they had lived in Paris .... 1980 .... 1995.
2. We have to be back from the party .... ten o'clock, so hurry up. (3)
3. What were you doing .... 9 p.m. .... Monday, June 22nd?
4. .... February we always go skiing .... a week.
5. Sally's friend Anna always comes .... December 26th, which is one day .... Christmas, and she stays .... January 3rd.
6. You mustn't play loud music or take a shower .... 10 p.m.
7. Last weekend my mum was so tired that she slept .... more than eight hours.
8. William Shakespeare died .... 1616. He was only 52 years old.
9. Aunt Liz and Uncle Tom have been here .... last Friday. They say they will stay .... next Thursday.
10. My parents bought this flat fifteen years ago. That was one year .... I was born.
11. We have been learning English .... more than six years now.
12. In Austria, children have to go to school .... six .... fifteen.
13. It was very late at night, certainly .... midnight, when the telephone rang.
14. Jim got up .... seven, so he was able to catch the early train.
15. We waited for our friends .... the sun had set.
16. I can't call you .... eight, because I will still be at football practice.
17. .... midnight the party was boring, but then it became really wild.
18. Boys, you have to hand in your projects .... next Monday, not one day later!
19. They told me they would get married .... August. Then they would go on honeymoon .... two weeks.
20. .... summer I go swimming, ... winter I ski as much as I can.
21. I've been at this school .... four years, and I'll stay .... next year.
22. Mum says we have to be back .... midnight. (3)
23. .... Bill went to Australia, he lived in Scotland.
24. Bill found a job with a computer company one week .... he arrived in Australia.
25. Richard will stay with us .... the next weekend.
26. My sister was born .... August 8th, exactly five years .... I was born.
27. I expect everyone to be here .... 10 o'clock sharp, not .... and not ....

58 Fill in suitable prepositions. Choose from the box.

Setze passende Vorwörter ein. Wähle von der "box" aus.

about – above – after – against – at – before – behind – below/beneath – beside/next to – by – for – from – in – into – of – on – over – to – under – while – with

1. Our cat is .... twelve years old, but we don't know exactly.
2. Larry, are you interested .... photography? – Sure! It's one of my hobbies.
3. How can Jack afford the new car? Its price was far .... his income.
4. The big mirror in the hall went .... pieces during the fight.
5. Boys will always be .... girls, that's a fact of life.
6. .... 200,000 people were .... the concert in Central Park.
7. We have nothing .... the new neighbours, although they are quite strange.
8. Many tourists are keen .... fish and chips when they come to England.
9. Today many people buy the things they need .... the supermarket.
10. You aren't afraid .... dogs, Maggie. Are you?
11. Don't forget to wash your hands .... you sit down to eat.
12. During our stay in London, Dad ran .... an old school friend.
13. My bus was ten minutes .... schedule again today. That's the third time this week.
14. The climbers were safe .... the cold in their tents.
15. I'm not going to argue with you, Jane. That's .... me.
16. We know .... sure that the dinosaurs were wiped out .... a meteor.
17. They are building a parking garage right .... the old church. How horrible!
18. My dad never talks on his mobile .... he is driving.
19. They did not walk .... day because it was too hot.
20. Jill was wearing only a T-shirt .... her jacket.
21. The dwarves in "Lord of the Ring" had their towns deep .... the mountains.
22. Nobody .... eighteen can buy alcohol in Britain, Ireland and the USA.
23. Old people often talk .... their health.
24. Homeless people often "live" .... bridges or .... the sewers.
25. In the army, a major is .... a lieutenant.
26. When I have a problem, I turn .... my friends .... help.
27. .... we had said our "good-byes", we went home.
28. Look at you! Your clothes are dirty all ....!
29. I was so angry that I threw my books .... the wall.
30. Gary is my best friend. I can always rely .... him.

31. We wanted to stay .... the "Hotel Central", but it was full.

32. Many famous painters worked in the South .... France for a while.

33. Mum had tidied up the whole house .... the visitors arrived.

34. Rafting was exciting, but we were never .... real danger.

35. Kylie ran so fast that she left all the other runners .... her.

36. Dad knows Mr. Greene .... work.

37. Daniel can stay .... the surface of the water for four minutes without breathing.

38. When do you usually leave .... school in the morning?

39. You can put the flowers .... the other presents.

40. Sabrina wants to dance only .... Daniel.

41. I always go to school .... bus.

42. Joe is .... trouble with his parents for lying .... an exam.

43. From the lighthouse we watched the fishing boats .... us.

44. These earrings belong .... my mother!

45. What's so funny, James? What are you laughing .... ?

46. Let's go camping again .... the weekend, shall we? (2)

47. On top of Mt. Everest, you are high .... all other mountain peaks.

48. Which shoes should I put .... ? – Well, it depends .... the weather.

49. Where's Sarah? – She's .... bed .... a bad cold.

50. Dad sometimes goes .... London .... business.

51. My parents are old-fashioned! They are completely .... techno music.

52. In the past, all ships were made .... wood.

53. Peter never looks .... me when I speak with him.

54. Mum got .... her car and drove .... work.

55. You should always read the fine print .... you sign anything.

56. We'll be there .... a minute. If not, please begin without us.

57. I don't want to sit .... Greg because he is so tall and I can't see the board.

58. After the dinner at the "Savoy", many people suffered .... diarrhea.

59. Water normally freezes when the temperature drops .... zero degrees.

60. Grandma has asked .... a glass of water. Can you get it .... her?

61. Who's this good-looking woman .... the headmaster? – That's his wife, I think.

62. Sandra always asks her dad .... money, never her mum.

63. This job should be done .... an expert.

64. My parents were taking a rest .... I was playing tennis with my sister.

59 Fill in suitable prepositions. "Everything goes!"

Setze passende Vorwörter ein. "Alles ist möglich!"

1. Look, there's a paraglider .... the sky, high .... the valley floor.
2. Let's go .... a walk, Teresa! – Okay, but what shall I put .... ?
3. As usual, the children went .... school .... foot.
4. Would you like mayonnaise .... your hamburger? – No, thanks. I'm not keen .... mayo. I prefer ketchup and mustard.
5. Dad wants to build a shed .... the garden .... the house.
6. I'm very interested .... foreign countries, but .... the present conditions I wouldn't travel .... some African countries.
7. In Canada summers can be quite warm, with temperatures .... 30°. But in winter they can drop to .... minus 30°.
8. Why are you .... such a hurry, Dad? – My train .... London leaves in 25 minutes, and it is always .... time.
9. Stop running .... girls like this, Bob! They will only laugh .... you.
10. I'm so sorry .... breaking the vase. I really didn't do it .... purpose.
11. Ian is going to marry Jenny. He says it was love .... first sight.
12. More and more people don't go skiing .... their winter holidays.
13. Dad was washing his car .... Dave and Sally were playing.
14. .... the way, have you ever asked your French teacher .... Paris?
15. I have been waiting .... you .... the corner of High Street and Market Street .... two o'clock. Where have you been?
16. These wonderful poems were written .... Shakespeare. They are called sonnets.
17. Some turtles can stay .... water .... hours.
18. The oldest Mexican pyramids are .... 1,000 years old, I think.
19. My dog gets very excited when a hot air balloon flies .... our house.
20. .... passing all his exams, Jack is looking forward .... his holidays.
21. Don't forget to take an umbrella .... you. It might rain later in the day.
22. The road was buried .... an avalanche, but luckily nobody was hurt.
23. Mark lives .... Manchester now. His family moved .... England .... 2005.
24. McDonald's can be found all .... the world.
25. Everybody congratulated me .... my fifteenth birthday.
26. You can really be proud .... your work, Melanie! It's excellent!

RELATIVE CLAUSES – Relativsätze

(a) *defining relative clauses* = einschränkende Relativsätze

- schränken die große Zahl der Möglichkeiten auf **eine Möglichkeit** ein;
- sind für das **Verstehen der Aussage** (des Hauptsatzes) erforderlich;
- kennen **keine Kommas** zwischen Hauptsatz und Relativsatz.

The people moved away a long time ago. They built this house.
***The people who built this house** moved away a long time ago.*

(b) *non-defining relative clauses* = erweiternde Relativsätze

- bieten **zusätzliche Informationen**, die unser Wissen erweitern;
- sind für das Verstehen der Aussage des Hauptsatzes **nicht erforderlich**;
- werden vom Hauptsatz durch **Kommas** getrennt.

John Smith moved away a long time ago. He built this house.
***John Smith, who built this house,** moved away a long time ago.*

▶▶ *relative pronouns*

who — für Personen; in **(a)** und **(b)** möglich
***The girls who** are standing over there are waiting for some friends.*
***Mary and Jane, who** are standing over there, are waiting for some friends.*

that — für Personen und Dinge; nur in **(a)** möglich ("Kein Komma vor *that*.")
*Who knows **the people that** live in the big house next to the church?*
***The big house that** (which) stands next to the church has new owners.*

which — für Dinge; in **(a)** und **(b)** möglich
***The road which** (that) passes by our house leads to Bristol.*
***Brazil, which** is South America's largest country, was settled by Portugal.*

which — für den ganzen Satz (nach einem Komma)
*Tim left the party early, **which** was the best thing he could do.*

whose — im zweiten Fall (*genitive*); für Personen und Dinge; in **(a)** und **(b)** möglich
*Is this **the boy whose** mother works in the school cafeteria?*
***Andre Agassi, whose** father is from Iran, was born in Las Vegas.*

what — = *that which (= was)*; kein Komma
*Jenny had no idea **what** she should do.*

no relative pronoun ("contact clause")
nur bei *"defining relative clauses"*; nur bei Bezug auf ein Objekt;
niemals anstelle von *"whose"*
***The boys ▼ we met** at Emma's party are very nice.* (statt *"who"/"that"*)
*I hate **the clothes ▼ Mum buys** for me.* (statt *"that"/"which"*)

60 Fill in the suitable relative pronoun or leave it out, and put commas if necessary.

Setze das passende Relativpronomen ein oder lasse es weg, und setze Kommas (in ☐), wo es nötig ist.

1. The yellow T-shirt ☐ .... was found in the dustbin last week ☐ belonged to Dave.
2. Children ☐ .... parents spend a lot of time with them ☐ are happier than others.
3. The boys ☐ .... you want to speak with ☐ are not here right now.
4. Dad, this is Mary ☐ .... has helped me a lot in the last few weeks.
5. In Chile, we often ate empanadas ☐ .... are a typical South American dish.
6. Argentina beat Mexico 3 to 1 ☐ .... is what everybody had expected.
7. They tried to swim across the river ☐ .... was a very silly idea.
8. The steaks ☐ .... we had for dinner last night ☐ were excellent.
9. People ☐ .... are able to speak a foreign language ☐ have better chances in life.
10. Beethoven's "Ninth Symphony" ☐ .... they are playing at the moment ☐ is the official European anthem.
11. A sculptor is an artist ☐ .... makes statues and monuments.
12. Please be quiet. I want to hear ☐ .... the man is saying.
13. Mrs. Walker ☐ .... always dyes her hair blonde ☐ thinks she looks like Madonna.
14. Everybody ☐ .... knows Margaret ☐ says that she is absolutely nice.
15. The Nile ☐ .... is one of the world's longest rivers ☐ comes from the Ethiopian Highlands.
16. Everybody wanted to know ☐ .... had happened at the party.
17. This is my mother's special apple strudel ☐ .... she has made especially for us.
18. Vanessa told Kevin a lot of things ☐ .... he did not want to hear.
19. Michael sometimes drinks when he drives ☐ .... will get him into trouble one day.
20. Ed has a very silly way of laughing ☐ .... everybody hates.
21. Plants ☐ .... grow in the jungle ☐ need a lot of heat and water.
22. I'd like to see "Alamo" ☐ .... tells the story of the fight between Mexico and Texas.
23. People ☐ .... are able to speak a foreign language have better chances in life.
24. Of all the cities ☐ .... I have seen I like Edinburgh best.
25. Claudia has about 150 DVDs ☐ .... is more than I have.
26. Uncle Walter ☐ .... lives in Philadelphia ☐ owns a restaurant.
27. How do you like the girls ☐ .... live next door?
28. Have you still got the stickers ☐ .... I gave you when we were in the 2nd form?
29. Dr. Jameson ☐ .... we have known for many years ☐ has opened an office in town.
30. The doctor ☐ .... put the plaster cast on my leg ☐ was very skilfull.
31. I like all the flowers ☐ .... grow in our garden.

32. We've never met the people ☐ .... guests we are tonight.

33. The policeman said, "I'd like to talk to the person ☐ .... drives the green Volvo ☐ .... is parked outside."

34. The black cat ☐ .... we used to feed every day ☐ hasn't shown up for some days now.

35. Aunt Annie always kisses me on the mouth ☐ .... I can't stand.

36. "Paintball" ☐ .... is a combat game ☐ looks dangerous but isn't really.

37. Dad never tells me ☐ .... he has to do for the company ☐ .... he works for.

38. Angela is the girl ☐ .... each of my friends would like to know better.

39. New York City ☐ .... is the largest city in the USA ☐ is not the country's capital.

40. The girl ☐ .... invited you to the party ☐ is my cousin Karen.

41. The Sun ☐ .... energy makes life on Earth possible ☐ is a relatively small star.

42. That's the boy ☐ .... cat has had six kittens.

43. Marcus ☐ .... cat has had six kittens ☐ is looking for homes for them.

44. The man ☐ .... car was stolen last Sunday ☐ has suffered a nervous breakdown.

45. Bennie had one hundred percent in his vocabulary test ☐ .... did not surprise anyone.

46. Joe bought the mountain bike from a boy ☐ .... family had moved to another city.

47. Our cinema is showing "War of the Worlds" ☐ .... is a film about an alien invasion.

48. The World Trade Center ☐ .... was destroyed on September 11, 2001 ☐ was also called the "Twin Towers" because it consisted of two very tall skyscrapers.

49. The boy ☐ .... is sitting next to me in class this year ☐ is my sister's boyfriend.

50. Why should we always do ☐ .... you want ☐ ?

51. The wine ☐ .... Dad bought last week ☐ was really expensive.

52. Mum did not believe my story ☐ .... made me very angry.

53. The earrings ☐ .... you found on the floor ☐ belonged to my mother.

54. The iPhone ☐ .... was on sale last month ☐ is sold out.

55. We paid 25,000 € for the car ☐ .... was not very much.

56. The bushes ☐ .... I planted in my garden last year ☐ are growing beautifully.

57. Nobody was there when I came into the room ☐ .... I found quite unusual.

58. The new cake ☐ .... Mum tried out on Saturday ☐ was rather disappointing.

59. The doctor ☐ .... you saw yesterday ☐ is my uncle.

60. We watched a video in our biology lesson ☐ .... was better than listening to the teacher.

61. Emily Dickinson ☐ .... wrote fascinating poetry ☐ was a remarkable woman.

62. The pictures ☐ .... you see on the wall ☐ were painted by my mum.

61 Connect the following sentences, forming relative clauses. (Mind the commas and leave out the relative pronoun if possible.)

Verbinde die folgenden Sätze, indem du Relativsätze bildest.
(Achte auf Kommas und auf die Möglichkeit, das Relativpronomen ganz wegzulassen.)

1. Our school team won the finals. Nobody really expected this.
2. The old man is an excellent accordion player. He often stands at the corner of our street.
3. Mr. Walker sometimes shows us videos. We like this very much.
4. Lake Superior is called "Oberer See" in German. It is the largest of the Great Lakes.
5. This is the family. Their house was destroyed by the fire.
6. The boys are not very clever. They are in our group this semester.
7. Lord Nelson defeated the French fleet in 1805. His tomb can be seen in St. Paul's Cathedral.
8. The physics book is quite difficult. I borrowed it from the library.
9. We saw a swallow in the middle of November. This is very unusual.
10. We had to throw away the mushrooms. We found them last weekend.
11. I think your mum is too old for the dress. She was wearing it at the garden party.
12. Luke likes heavy metal. His parents don't really understand it.
13. John Lennon was killed by a madman. He was one of the Beatles.
14. The boys will be punished. They threw something at their teacher.
15. Our neighbours returned from Croatia a week sooner. This surprised us all.
16. The Bergers found oil on their land. This made them very rich.
17. Yuri Gagarin was a very humble person. His space flight surprised everyone.
18. The man survived. He was struck by lightning. This was like a miracle.
19. My girlfriend has no time for me. Her relatives from Canada are visiting at the moment.
20. Mario won't be in my class next year. This makes me quite sad.
21. Los Angeles has more Hispanics than any other city in the USA. We are going to visit it next month.
22. Everybody hates Mrs. Manning. They know her well.
23. My mum often makes pizza. It is my favourite dish.
24. They gave the medal to the policeman. He had saved a young man from drowning.
25. Many important people have received the Nobel Peace Prize. It is presented by the Norwegian King.
26. The car is a Toyota. My dad is driving it at the moment.
27. This morning I missed my bus. This made me be late for school.
28. Austria beat Germany. Nobody really expected that.
29. Look, there's the boy. We met his sister at Marvin's party.
30. The DVDs were rather cheap. Martin bought them on the internet.
31. My parents can be quite strict sometimes. They are usually rather lenient.
32. J. K. Rowling is Britain's richest woman. You like her books so much.
33. My sister came home at 2 o'clock last night. This made my parents very angry.
34. Is this the house? Do you want to look at it?
35. Belvedere Castle in Vienna is very beautiful. It was built for Prince Eugene of Savoy.
36. Tony had no idea. What should he do?
37. Muhammad Ali died in 2016. His birth name was Cassius Marcellus Clay.
38. I took the photo. It won the first prize.

REPORTED/INDIRECT SPEECH – Indirekte Rede

(a) *statements* = Aussagen

reporting verbs ▶

add	=	hinzufügen
admit	=	zugeben, gestehen
agree	=	zustimmen, einverstanden sein
answer	=	antworten, erwidern
claim	=	behaupten, fordern
complain	=	sich beklagen
confess	=	zugeben, gestehen
explain	=	erklären
know	=	wissen
promise	=	versprechen
remark	=	bemerken, anmerken
reply	=	erwidern, antworten
say	=	sagen
think	=	denken, glauben
to be sure	=	(sich) sicher sein, gewiss sein

(b) *questions* = Fragen

reporting verbs ▶

ask	=	fragen
enquire	=	(nach)fragen
want to know	=	wissen wollen
wonder	=	wissen wollen, neugierig sein

- ***questions with question words*** → ***same word is used in reported question***
  - ***Who** are you?* → *I wanted to know **who** she was.*
  - ***How** do you feel?* → *They asked me **how** I felt.*
  - ***When** will you call?* → *Sue wondered **when** I would call.*

- ***questions without questions words = general questions*** → ***"if"/"whether"***
  - ***Is** Willie happy?* → *We wondered **whether** Willie was happy.*
  - ***Can** you see anything?* → *Joe asked me **if** I could see anything.*
  - ***Do** you believe me?* → *Tina wanted to know **if** we believed her.*

(c) *commands* = Befehle

reporting verbs ▶

advise	=	raten
ask	=	bitten
command	=	befehlen, anschaffen
expect	=	erwarten
order	=	befehlen
tell	=	sagen, befehlen

- ***with the infinitive***
  - ***Bring** me a coke!* → *Joe told me **to bring** him a coke.*
  - ***Don't look** at me!* → *Stella asked me **not to look** at her.*

- ***with "should (not)"***
  - ***Bring** me a coke!* → *Joe said **I should bring** him a coke.*
  - ***Don't look** at me!* → *Stella said **we shouldn't look** at her.*

▶▶ ***Reporting verb in present tense (or future tense or present perfect tense):***

NO CHANGE OF TENSES!!

*"My dad **works** in a car shop."*	→	*Alex **tells** me that his dad **works** in a car shop.*
*"I'll **call** you soon."*	→	*Gina **has promised** that she **will call** me soon.*
*"We **met** Leah in Rio."*	→	*Joe **will say** they **met** Leah in Rio.*
*"Where **have** you **been**?"*	→	*Mum **wonders** where I **have been.***
▼		▼ ▼
"original tense"		***"present group"*** ***"same tense"***

▶▶ ***Reporting verb in past tense (or past perfect tense):***

CHANGE OF TENSES!!

direct speech	→	***reported/indirect speech***
present tense	→	*past tense*
past tense	→	*past perfect tense*
present perfect tense	→	*past perfect tense*
"will"-future	→	*1st conditional ("would + infinitive")*

Die anderen Zeiten bleiben unverändert!

*"My dad **works** in a car shop."*	→	*Alex **told** me that his dad **worked** in a car shop.*
*"I'll **call** you soon."*	→	*Gina **promised** that she **would call** me soon.*
*"We **met** Leah in Rio."*	→	*Joe **said** they **had met** Leah in Rio.*
*"Where **have** you been?"*	→	*Mum **wondered** where I **had been**.*
▼		▼ ▼
"original tense"		***"past group"*** ***"different tense"***

62 Put the following sentences into reported speech (reporting verbs in past group).

Setze die folgenden Sätze in die indirekte Rede (einleitende Verben in past tense).

<u>example:</u> "What are you doing here? I've told you I don't want to see you again." ▶
Max asked what I was doing there; he had told me he didn't want to see me again.

1. Can I speak with you? I have to ask you an important question.
2. I know I've made a bad mistake. Can you forgive me one more time?
3. What did Joe tell you about me? Do you believe him?
4. I've been looking for you all day. Where have you been?
5. You are such a clever person. Why can't you take the test instead of me?
6. A girl has asked for you three times today. Is she your new girlfriend?
7. Mum, can I stay out till midnight? I want to go to a concert with Fred.
8. Have you seen Mr. Solomon's new car? Where did he get the money for it?
9. When did you get here? I didn't hear you come in.
10. Simon's sister is very pretty. Do you know her?
11. Go away! I don't want to see you.
12. Why do you always do such silly things? They are dangerous.
13. You should tell your parents about the incident. Why haven't you done so already?
14. How did you find out my new address? Nobody knows about it.
15. Meet me in the park this afternoon. I want to speak with you.
16. Will you bring Monica to my party with you? I want to meet her.
17. I wasn't lend you my car. Do you think I'm crazy?
18. Don't say anything right now! You can only make things worse than they are.
19. Why are you lying to me? Everybody knows that you took Joe's CD player.
20. Nancy isn't in her room. Do you know where she is?
21. I'm worried about my grandma. She hasn't called or written for two weeks.
22. Are you alright, Mrs. Winters? We can do the shopping for you.
23. You should not touch this animal. It may be ill.
24. Send your father to me tomorrow! I've had enough of your silly ideas.
25. Who will pay for the group? I haven't got enough money with me.
26. Germany will lose the finals. Are you going to watch the match on TV?
27. Go home immediately! There has been a bomb threat at school.
28. Ms. Jenkins is busy. You can't see her today. Why didn't you call and make an appointment?
29. I want you to meet my parents this weekend. Can you come on Saturday?
30. Can you come again tomorrow? I can't speak with you tonight because we have guests.
31. What will you tell your friends? They will be disappointed if they find out the truth.
32. How did you solve these problems? Did you ask anyone for help?
33. Will you be at Oliver's party? I don't think I'll go this time.
34. Please show me the way to the cafeteria! I'm new at this school.
35. Where shall we put the fridge? Have you made room for it?
36. Your letter has not reached me yet. When did you send it?
37. How fast can your car go? My dad's Aston Martin can do 300 kilometres per hour.
38. Is it true that you've won the first prize? I read about it in yesterday's paper.
39. Mario has hurt his leg. Will he be able to play next weekend?

STYLE & VOCABULARY – Stil & Wortschatz

(A) BRINGEN

- ***bring – brought – brought*** ▶ **"herbringen" = hin zum Sprecher**

*Please **bring** me some stamps from the post office.*
*Look what I **have brought** you! Fresh cherries!*
*A doctor: "Today they **brought** three people to the hospital after an accident."*

- ***take – took – taken*** ▶ **"hinbringen" = vom Sprecher weg**

*Can you **take** the books to the library for me, please?*
*Who **will take** the letters to the post office today?*
*The ambulance driver: "Today I **took** three people to the hospital after an accident."*

(B) GEBEN

- ***give – gave – given*** ▶ **jemand etwas geben; von Mensch zu Mensch**

*Please **give me** a bottle of milk, six eggs and a pound of butter.*
*Who **gave you** this book? I've always wanted to read it.*
*The tour guide **has given us** all the information we need.*

- ***put – put – put*** ▶ **etwas (ein Ding) wohin geben (legen, stellen)**

*Where shall **I put the shopping**, Mum? – On the kitchen table, please.*
*You should **put your papers** away, Tom, or you won't find them.*
*Paul always **puts his dirty socks** on my bed, and I hate it!*

(C) FAHREN

- ***go – went – gone*** ▶ **für "reisen" allgemein; sich von A nach B bewegen**

*We often **go** to Greece in summer.* (kann "fahren", "fliegen" ... bedeuten)
*Lisa **went to** Scotland last year.* (wieder allgemein; kann Verschiedenes meinen)
*When **will we go** to the USA, Mum?* (siehe oben)

- ***drive – drove – driven*** ▶ **selbst mit dem Auto (Bus, LKW ...) fahren; ≠ *ride***

*My dad **drives** a BMW now.* (Er ist der Fahrer.)
*Mum **drove** us to school today.* (Sie ist gefahren, wir sind mitgefahren.)
***Will** you **drive** to Greece or fly?* (Selbst fahren oder fliegen?)

- ***ride – rode – ridden*** ▶ **mitfahren, nicht selbst lenken (Auto, Zug, Bus); ≠ *drive***
  ▶ **mit dem Rad (Motorrad) fahren oder mitfahren**

*The first 100 miles I drive, you **ride**.* (Ich lenke, du sitzt daneben.)
*Fewer and fewer people **ride** the train to work.*
*Dad likes to **ride** his motorbike, and Mum **rides** with him.*

63 Fill in the correct words.
Setze die richtigen Wörter ein.

1. My parents believe that (*fahren*) .... a moped is too dangerous.
2. Have you (*gegeben*) .... the flowers into the vase, Anita?
3. Peter, will you (*bringen*) .... the wastepaper basket downstairs?
4. My dad has to (*fahren*) .... to England twice a month.
5. Waiter, please (*bringen*) .... me a glass of orange juice.
6. When I'm eighteen, my parents will let me (*fahren*) .... our car, I hope.
7. I don't like (*mitfahren*) .... in a car with David because he usually (*fährt*) .... too fast for me.
8. Mum, can you (*bringen*) .... me to school tomorrow morning?
9. When it's not too hot, I (*fahre*) .... my bike for an hour or so every day.
10. My grandma (*gab*) .... me 50 € for my school report and I (*brachte*) .... the money to the bank at once.
11. When I broke my arm last year, my dad (*brachte*) .... me to the hospital, and there the doctors (*gaben*) .... a plaster cast on my arm.
12. Did you (*geben*) .... the books on the shelf, as I told you? – No, I didn't. I (*gab*) .... them to Mike. He said he would do it.
13. My dad usually (*fährt*) .... his car to work, but sometimes he (*fährt*) .... the bus.
14. Children believe that Santa Claus (*bringt*) .... the presents at Christmas.
15. Santa Claus (*gibt*) .... the presents into the socks at the foot of the bed.
16. Dad, can you (geben) .... me some money? My friends and I are (*fahren*) .... to the zoo tomorrow.
17. Children, (*gebt*) .... your books away and open your test books.
18. Mum (*brachte*) .... her car to the garage because it had a flat tyre.
19. (*fahren*) .... the bus is a lot cheaper than (*fahren*) .... a car, but it's less comfortable.
20. Who has (*gegeben*) .... these photos on the internet? They are terrible!
21. Dad (*brachte*) .... Mum some tea from England.
22. Our friends (*gaben*) .... us this CD so that we can remember their visit.
23. Let's (*fahren*) ....! It's late and I don't want you to (*fahren*) .... too fast.
24. (*bringe*) .... these papers to the headmaster, please.

(D) LASSEN

• ***let – let – let***	▶	**zulassen, erlauben, gestatten**
*Please **let** me in! It's cold outside.*		(Bitte lasse es zu!)
*Joe **let** us use his DVD player.*		(Er erlaubte uns die Benutzung.)
*I **won't let** you go away!*		(Ich gestatte es nicht.)
• ***make – made – made***	▶	**veranlassen, zwingen, dazu bringen**
*Mr. Milk often **makes** me get angry.*		(Er lässt mich oft zornig werden.)
*Please don't **make** us say it again!*		(Zwing uns nicht, es noch einmal zu sagen.)
*You can't **make** me stay here!*		(Du wirst mich nicht dazu bringen.)
• ***leave – left – left***	▶	**übrig lassen (so lassen, wie es ist, zurücklassen)**
*I think I've **left** my books at home.*		(Ich habe meine Bücher daheim gelassen.)
*You never **leave** anything for me.*		(Du lässt mir nie etwas übrig.)
*Please **leave** the money on the desk.*		(Lass das Geld auf dem Tisch liegen.)
• ***[have] + object + 3rd form***	▶	**jemand etwas machen lassen; es nicht selbst tun**
*Joe **has his hair cut** every month.*		(Er lässt sich jeden Monat die Haare schneiden.)
*Sue **had the dress made** in Paris.*		(Sie ließ sich das Kleid in Paris machen.)
*I'**ll have the photos developed** soon.*		(Ich werde die Fotos bald entwickeln lassen.)

▶▶▶ ACHTUNG! Nicht verwechseln mit ...

Joe has cut his hair.	→	Er hat sich die Haare (selbst) geschnitten.
Sue had made the dress.	→	Sie hatte das Kleid (selbst) gemacht.
I'll develop the photos.	→	Ich werde die Fotos (selbst) entwickeln.

• ***Some phrases with "lassen" in German and in English:***

Lass ihn (gehen, schlafen ...).	→	***Let** him (go, sleep ...).*
Lass mich sehen!	→	***Let** me see!*
Lasst sie reden!	→	***Let** them talk!*
Lass mich das machen!	→	***Let** me do it!*
Lass dich nicht stören.	→	***Don't let** me (them ...) disturb you.*
Bitte lass mich in Ruhe! (... in Frieden)	→	*Please **leave** me **alone**! (... **in peace**!)*
Überlasst das mir!	→	***Leave** it to me!*
Lass alles so, wie es ist.	→	***Leave** everything as it is.*
Sie ließen alle Türen und Fenster offen.	→	*They **left** all the doors and windows **open**.*
Du musst das alles hinter dir lassen.	→	*You must **leave** all this **behind** (you).*
Wer hat den Fernseher angelassen?	→	*Who has **left** the TV **on**?*
Lass das sein! (= Hör auf damit!)	→	***Stop it**! / **That's enough**!*
Nicht fallen lassen!	→	*Don't **drop** it!*
Lasst es euch schmecken!	→	***Enjoy**!*
Das hätte ich mir nie träumen lassen!	→	*I never dreamed **it was possible**.*
Ich muss mir einen Zahn ziehen lassen.	→	*I must **have** a tooth **(taken) out**.*
Wir ließen einen Installateur kommen.	→	*We **sent for** a plumber.*
Bitte lass mich nicht warten!	→	*Please don't **keep** me waiting!*
Ich habe mir sagen lassen, dass ...	→	*I've **heard** that ... / I've **been told** that ...*
Lass dir Zeit!	→	***Take** your **time**!*
Ich lasse euch fünf Minuten Zeit.	→	*I'll **give** you five minutes.*
Joe lässt sich einen Bart wachsen.	→	*Joe **is growing** a beard.*

64 Translate these "*lassen*"-sentences into good English.

Übersetze diese "lassen"-Sätze in gutes Englisch.

1. Vater hat seine Aktentasche im Büro gelassen.
2. Lass diesen Unsinn, Kevin!
3. Meine Eltern lassen mich unter der Woche nicht fernsehen.
4. Walter ließ sich sein Auto schwarz lackieren.
5. Jemand hat das Licht angelassen!
6. Bitte lassen Sie uns heute früher nachhause gehen.
7. Warum lässt du uns immer so lange warten?
8. Mein Opa ließ sich seine Anzüge von einem Freund machen.
9. Meine Mutter lässt mich immer am Wochenende mein Zimmer aufräumen.
10. Lass mich nachdenken!
11. Ich glaube, du kannst den Fall mir überlassen.
12. Bitte lass mich hier nicht allein zurück!
13. Gerald kann es nicht lassen – er muss immer das neueste Handy haben!
14. Mr. Smith ließ uns die ganze Übung noch einmal schreiben.
15. Es ist erst vier Uhr. Das heißt, wir können uns Zeit lassen.
16. Warum ist die Vase kaputt? – Fred hat sie fallen gelassen.
17. Ich werde euch nicht gehen lassen, bevor ihr meine Fragen beantwortet.
18. Lass die Kinder in Ruhe, Mike. Sie wollen spielen.
19. Es tut mir leid, dass ich Sie warten ließ.
20. Hast du mir etwas Orangensaft übrig gelassen?
21. Hier ist die Nachspeise! Lass sie dir schmecken!
22. Lass mich das nicht noch einmal sagen!
23. Die Stadtverwaltung lässt die alten Bäume umschneiden.
24. Ihr könnt eure Schuhe anlassen.
25. Lass deine Disketten nicht überall herumliegen!
26. Wir ließen London hinter uns und fuhren weiter in Richtung Wales.
27. Meine Eltern ließen einen Elektriker kommen.
28. Ich überlasse es dir, ob du kommen willst oder nicht.
29. Lasst uns gehen! Wir haben genug gesehen.
30. Mein Vater ließ die Pläne von einem Freund zeichnen.
31. Schau, Ines hat sich die Haare schneiden lassen!
32. Diese Bilder lassen mich immer über die Not in der Welt nachdenken.
33. Oh nein! Ich habe meine Englischbücher in der Schule gelassen!
34. Mrs. Carter sagt, sie lässt uns eine Woche Zeit für den Aufsatz.
35. Ich habe mir sagen lassen, dass Madrid eine tolle Stadt ist.
36. Mein Bruder lässt sich oft Bücher aus England schicken.
37. Der Bauer ließ uns das Zelt auf seiner Wiese aufstellen.
38. Wo hast du denn heute deine Freunde gelassen?
39. Warum lässt du mir die Fotos nicht anschauen?
40. Nach dem Unfall musste ich mir zwei Zähne ziehen lassen.
41. Unsere Nachbarn lassen ihr Auto immer vor dem Haus stehen.

(E) „MAN"

- ***you – we – they – people***

In English ***you*** *say "Pardon?" for "Wie bitte?"*
Auf Englisch sagt <u>man</u> "Pardon?" für "Wie bitte?"

In Austria ***we*** *say "Mahlzeit!" before a meal.*
In Österreich sagt <u>man</u> (= sagen wir) "Mahlzeit" vor dem Essen.

They *will finish the new sports centre in three years.*
<u>Man</u> wird das neue Sportzentrum in drei Jahren fertig stellen.

People *say that Paris is more elegant than London.*
Man sagt, Paris sei eleganter als London.

- ***passive voice***

Spanish and Portuguese ***are spoken*** *in South America.*
In Südamerika spricht <u>man</u> Spanisch und Portugiesisch.

Butter ***is made*** from milk.
Butter macht <u>man</u> aus Milch.

We ***were told*** *to wait outside.*
<u>Man</u> sagte uns, wir sollen draußen warten.

It ***is believed*** *that the Vikings reached North America 500 years before Columbus.*
<u>Man</u> glaubt, die Wikinger hätten Nordamerika 500 Jahre vor Kolumbus erreicht.

65 Translate these "*man*"-sentences into good English.
Übersetze diese "man"-Sätze in gutes Englisch.

1. In Japan zieht man sich die Schuhe aus, wenn man ein Haus betritt.
2. Zu Weichnachten gibt man viel Geld für Geschenke aus.
3. New York City nennt man auch "The Big Apple".
4. Man spielt im Sommer nicht Eishockey.
5. Man hat uns gesagt, wir sollen keinen Lärm machen.
6. Im Winter bezahlt man mehr für ein Zimmer als im Sommer.
7. Ich bin sicher, man wird das Problem bald lösen.
8. Englisch spricht man auf der ganzen Welt.
9. Man darf die Straße hier nicht überqueren.
10. In Österreich ist man sehr stolz auf die Schimannschaft.
11. Man hat ein sehr strenges Gesetz gegen das Rauchen beschlossen.
12. Wann wird man hier endlich einen Zebrastreifen machen?
13. Man sagt, dass Fischen sehr entspannend sein kann.
14. Man bat uns, den Raum nicht zu verlassen.
15. Zu älteren Menschen sollte man besonders höflich sein.
16. Man muss drei Formulare ausfüllen, bevor man in die USA einreisen darf.
17. Man weiß nicht sicher, wo die ersten Menschen gelebt haben.
18. Man soll immer "bitte" und "danke" sagen.

19. Weihnachten verbringt man üblicherweise mit seiner Familie.
20. Man nennt William Shakespeare auch "The Swan of Avon".
21. In den arabischen Ländern geht man am Freitag in die Moschee.
22. In vielen Ländern isst man kein Schweinefleisch.
23. Man hat uns nicht zu der Feier eingeladen.
24. Man soll immer anklopfen, bevor man eintritt.
25. Bei uns trinkt man mehr Kaffee als Tee.
26. In den USA isst man zu Thanksgiving meist Truthahn.
27. Man sagt, Pelé sei der beste Fußballspieler aller Zeiten.
28. Man darf nicht zu oft zu spät kommen.
29. Letztes Jahr hat man die Hauptstraße repariert.
30. Man weiß, dass Wasser schwerer als Öl ist.
31. Man muss die Tiere einmal pro Tag füttern.
32. Man erhebt sich, wenn die Hymnen gespielt werden.
33. In Großbritannien gibt man sich nicht so oft die Hand wie in Österreich.
34. Man spricht nicht schlecht über andere hinter ihrem Rücken.
35. Man darf dieses Zimmer nicht betreten.
36. Manchmal muss man alte Gebäude niederreißen.
37. Man schreibt Hausübungen nicht ab; man schreibt sie selbst.
38. Mit Fremden spricht man nicht!
39. Man soll immer nachdenken, bevor man handelt.
40. Zu Ostern bemalt und versteckt man Eier.
41. Man glaubt, dass es irgendwo noch Saurier gibt.
42. In diesem Beruf kann man viel Geld verdienen.
43. Man weiß nicht wirklich, wie viel Geld das neue Rathaus kosten wird.
44. Man soll in der Schule immer aufpassen.
45. Im Herbst soll man nicht ohne Regenschirm aus dem Haus gehen.
46. In Ostasien isst man Hunde.
47. Da muss man etwas dagegen tun!
48. Am Morgen und am Abend putzt man sich die Zähne.
49. In manchen Ländern feiert man Weihnachten erst im Jänner.
50. Man hat die Schlösser ausgetauscht, während wir weg waren.
51. In der Schweiz spricht man vier Sprachen.
52. Man weiß, dass Harry gern schnell fährt.
53. Im Park darf man die Wiesen nicht betreten.
54. Man darf nicht alles glauben, was in den Zeitungen steht.
55. Man hat mich erst gestern informiert.
56. Vom Fenster aus konnte man die Parade gut beobachten.
57. Man versucht, Drogenhändler von Schulen fernzuhalten.
58. In vielen Gegenden geht man am Sonntag zur Kirche.
59. Man behauptet, dass du eine gute Tänzerin bist.
60. Man darf exotische Tiere nicht mit ins Land bringen.
61. Man hätte uns rechtzeitig informieren sollen.
62. Man hält meinen Vater für einen sehr klugen Menschen.

(F) SAGEN

- *say – said – said*

▶ **ohne Person: "etwas sagen", "sprechen"**

*Frank **said** that he had seen a UFO the night before.*
*What did Nancy **say** when she saw the presents?*
*Mark was so angry that he didn't know what to **say**.*

▶ **mit Person: "etwas zu jemand sagen" ▶ *"say to"***

*Jenny **said to me** that she wanted to be my girlfriend.*
*What can I **say to you** so that you believe me?*
*Why do you **say** such things **to me**?*

▶ ***Some phrases with "say":***

***To say nothing of** …*	→	ganz zu schweigen von …
*I've **nothing to say for** myself.*	→	Ich habe nichts zu meiner Verteidigung zu sagen.
***The article** (book …) **says** …*	→	In dem Artikel (Buch …) steht …
***The weather report says** …*	→	Der Wetterbericht besagt …
***It says here that** …*	→	Hier steht, dass …
***My watch says** half past two.*	→	Auf meiner Uhr ist es halb drei.
***They say** you are the best.*	→	Man sagt, du seist der/die Beste.
***You are said** to be the best.*	→	Man sagt / Es heißt, du seist der/die Beste.
You don't say!	→	No sowas! Was du nicht sagst!
that is to say	→	das heißt
***Let us say** he likes it.*	→	Angenommen, es gefällt ihm.
You may well say so.	→	Das kann man wohl sagen.
It's hard to say.	→	Es ist schwer zu sagen.
It goes without saying that …	→	Es ist selbstverständlich, dass …
say a prayer / poem	→	ein Gebet sprechen / Gedicht aufsagen
What are you saying?	→	Was meinst du denn?
That's not for (me) to say.	→	Das kann (ich) nicht entscheiden!
*Is Sue nice? – **I should say so!***	→	Na und ob! Na und wie!
***There is no saying** what will happen.*	→	Man weiß nie, was passieren wird.

- *tell – told – told* ▶ **immer mit einer Person, aber ohne "*to*"**

*Frank **told us** that he had seen a UFO the night before.*
*What did Nancy **tell you** about the presents?*
*Mark was so angry that he didn't know what to **tell his teacher**.*
*How much will you **tell your parents** about the whole thing?*
*Nobody **told me** that Joe would be at the party too.*
*I could **tell them** a thing or two about this man!*

▶ ***Some phrases with "tell":***

I have been told …	→	Man hat mir gesagt/mitgeteilt …
I told you so!	→	Das habe ich dir ja gleich gesagt!
*I ('ll) **tell you what!***	→	Ich sag' dir was! Weißt du was?
***I can tell by your looks** that …*	→	Ich kann an deinem Aussehen erkennen, dass …
***You can tell that** he is sorry.*	→	Man sieht es ihm an, dass es ihm leid tut.
You must do as you are told.	→	Du musst tun, was man dir sagt.
***All told**, I liked the story.*	→	Alles in allem gefällt mir die Geschichte.
*Can you **tell** me **the time**?*	→	Kannst du mir sagen, wie spät es ist?
*I **told** them **the way**.*	→	Ich habe ihnen den Weg erklärt.

You never can tell.	→	Man kann nie wissen.
How can I tell?	→	Wie/Woher soll ich das wissen?
more than words can tell	→	mehr, als man mit Worten sagen kann
tell the difference / tell apart	→	den Unterschied feststellen, auseinanderhalten
tell A from B	→	A von B unterscheiden
tell on someone	→	jemand verpetzen/verraten
Don't tell!	→	Nichts sagen! Nicht verraten!
tell a lie	→	lügen
tell a secret	→	ein Geheimnis verraten
tell a story	→	eine Geschichte erzählen
tell the truth	→	die Wahrheit sagen

66 Fill in the correct forms of "say" and "tell".

Setze die richtigen Formen von "say" und "tell" ein.

1. Dad .... that he had left his briefcase at the office last night.
2. My brother is only three years old, but he can already .... the time.
3. You must .... me the truth! Did you kiss my boyfriend or didn't you?
4. The man on the radio .... that there will be rain the next few days.
5. Look at Rosie! You can .... that she doesn't feel comfortable.
6. Come on, ... us! What did Mr. Chambers .... to you?
7. Joe's train arrives at 6 o'clock. That is to .... in three hours.
8. What did you .... to him? Did you .... him your name?
9. You should read this article, Dad. It .... that teens work harder than adults.
10. We have been .... to come again at seven o'clock tomorrow morning.
11. Who has .... you this story? It sounds like fantasy to me.
12. Did you .... your parents about the Maths test? – Yes, I did. My dad .... that it was very easy and he can't understand why I got a "C".
13. Everybody .... that the new pizzeria is wonderful!
14. I can never .... Peter from Michael. I think they look exactly alike.
15. The latest "Star Wars" film has its ups and downs, but all ...., it is quite good.
16. Let us .... your dad finds out about the broken window. What will you .... him?
17. The tour guide .... that the Tower of London was once used as a prison.
18. He also .... us that the men in the funny uniforms are called "Beefeaters".
19. I'll .... you what! Let's call Tim and Fred and have a party!
20. England and Ireland are .... to be very expensive at the moment.
21. When I was young, I always had to .... a poem on Mother's Day.
22. Can I .... you a secret? But you must promise to keep it to yourself!

23. How can I .... if Betty likes me? – Well, you could ask her!
24. Did you like your skiing trip? – I should .... so! It was perfect!
25. Nobody .... us that they were going to dig up the street in front of the house.
26. "Sagen" can mean "say" or "tell". How can you .... the difference?
27. Have you heard? Mary and Colin are going to get married! – You don't ....! I spoke with Colin yesterday, but he didn't .... anything about it to me.
28. It .... here that the Americans are planning to send a space ship to Mars.
29. It's hard to .... which is the best football team at the moment. Brazil, perhaps.
30. Mr. Kemp is .... to be an excellent teacher.
31. Soldiers must always do what they are ....
32. A friendly shopkeeper .... us the way to the museum.
33. Is Dad driving to work this morning? – Yes, he is. He .... me so last night.
34. You can .... the boys they need not wait for me after school today.
35. I think your plans are okay, but it's not for me to ....!
36. How can the headmaster know all this? Somebody must have .... him!
37. Martina is a real teacher's pet! She always .... on other pupils!
38. When I was at primary school, we always .... a prayer in the morning.
39. The weather report .... there will be lots of sunshine tomorrow and no rain, but with the weather in the mountains you never can ....
40. We have been .... that Mr. Jenkins lives here. Is this true?
41. Oscar is a liar and a thief! – Well, I .... you so, but you didn't believe me.
42. What's the matter, Phil? I can .... by your looks that something is wrong.
43. If you don't want to go out with me, ... so and I won't ask you again.
44. Veronica has .... me that you are always taking her things. What have you got to .... to this?
45. Did you give them my phone number? – No, and I didn't .... them your name, either.
46. Liz .... that she'd broken up with Ian, but she didn't .... me why. – You don't ....! They seemed so happy together!
47. It's difficult to .... anything positive about Malcolm. He is arrogant and rude, and he thinks he knows everything. – Yes, and they .... he's a liar too.
48. Let's go to the cinema tonight! It goes without .... that I'll pay for the tickets.
49. Everybody .... me that Beyoncé's latest CD is great, but I must .... that I don't really like it.
50. We'll visit New York again next summer; that is to .... in half a year.

51. Cindy, you promised me you would not .... anybody about our plans, and now everybody knows about them! – But I swear I didn't .... anything!
52. It's easy to .... the difference between a good team and a bad one.
53. Excuse me, can you .... me what time it is? – Sure! It's ten to eight.
54. Something is wrong with Sarah. You can .... that she has problems.
55. How can you .... that I haven't .... you the truth? You should know that I never .... lies!
56. Let's .... you are right! Then we should .... your parents.
57. Let's try this jam. They .... it is the best!
58. Why didn't you .... me earlier that you need some money?
59. You never can .... whether Joe is joking or not.
60. Does your dad like the new car? – I should .... so! It was expensive enough!
61. I think we should stop the project now, but that's not for me to ....
62. What have you got to .... for yourselves, boys? Did you break the window or didn't you? – We didn't do it, sir. That's all we can .... about it.
63. We should inform the police, although there is no .... what they will do.
64. It goes without .... that everybody has to tidy up their own rooms.
65. In April, you can never .... what the weather will be like.
66. It's important that children learn to .... right from wrong.
67. .... them to go away, please! I don't want to see them now.
68. Don't always ask why, just do what I .... you!
69. Sally is terrible! She likes .... lies, even about her best friends.
70. "If you .... me the truth, nothing will happen to you", the detective .... to the boys.
71. I hate it when people .... "I .... you so!"
72. I'll .... you what we'll do; we'll .... we were late because the bus didn't arrive on time.
73. It's easy to .... us apart: I have blue eyes, my brother has brown eyes.
74. My watch .... it's twelve o'clock, but what time is it really?
75. That's interesting! It .... here that dolphins have bigger brains than people.
76. Bob says he won a million Pounds, but it goes without .... that he's lying.
77. On every cigarette box it ...., "Smoking can kill!"
78. Who .... you about my accident? – I read about it in the newspaper. The article .... that a car knocked you off your bike.

(G) SOLLEN

- ***shall*** ► **in Fragen und Verboten**

__Shall__ I go or __shall__ I stay? → Soll ich gehen oder soll ich bleiben?

Where __shall__ we put the books? → Wohin sollen wir die Bücher legen?

You __shall not__ spend more money than you earn.
→ Du sollst nicht mehr Geld ausgeben, als du verdienst.

The Bible says, "You __shall not__ kill!"
→ Die Bibel sagt: "Du sollst nicht töten!"

- ***should / ought to*** ► **"sollte"; meist ein Rat oder Tipp**

It's late. I think you __should / ought__ to go home.
→ Es ist spät. Ich glaube, du solltest nachhause gehen.

If you have a problem, you __should / ought to__ speak with your parents.
→ Wenn du Probleme hast, solltest du mit deinen Eltern sprechen.

You __shouldn't / ought not to__ spend so much money on sweets.
→ Du solltest nicht so viel Geld für Süßigkeiten ausgeben.

__Should__ we / __Ought__ we __to__ walk or take the bus?
→ Soll(t)en wir zu Fuß gehen oder mit dem Bus fahren?

- ***to be (supposed) to + infinitive*** ► **es wird erwartet, dass es so ist**

We __are supposed to be__ back by midnight. = We __are to be__ back by midnight.
→ Wir sollen spätestens um Mitternacht zurück sein.
(= Es wird von uns erwartet.)

You __are not supposed to know__ about this plan.
→ Du sollst gar nichts von diesem Plan wissen.
(= Niemand will, dass du etwas davon weißt.)

__Am__ I __supposed to do__ everything by myself? = __Am__ I __to do__ everything by myself?
→ Soll ich alles allein/selbst machen?
(= Wird das von mir erwartet?)

- ***"Do you want (me) + infinitive"*** ► **„Soll ich ... ?" (Möchtest du, dass ...?)**

__Do you want me to help__ you with the cooking?
→ Soll ich dir beim Kochen helfen? (Möchtest du, dass ich dir ...?)

__Do you want us to start__ now?
→ Sollen wir jetzt anfangen?

__Do you want Mr. Jones to call__ again tomorrow?
→ Soll Mr. Jones morgen wieder anrufen?

67 Fill in the correct forms of *"sollen"*.

Setze die richtigen Formen von "sollen" ein.

1. .... we begin now or .... we wait a bit?
2. .... we really do this?
3. You .... be quiet now, boys. The film has begun.
4. You .... not steal!
5. .... I switch off the lights or do you want to read a little longer?
6. What a disaster! We .... have known this would go wrong.
7. At your age you .... be smarter!
8. I'm sure you'll make it. You .... not even think of failing!
9. The boys .... stop playing now and come in.
10. ....n't you go to bed now? It's already past ten o'clock.
11. What .... I say? I think it's not a good idea to go out with John.
12. I know I .... not be here, but I've missed the bus.
13. Dad says we .... ask you, Mum.
14. I think you .... take a shower, Benny. You smell!
15. You .... do what your parents say.
16. Mike .... not drink so much. He always has bleary eyes.
17. You .... have asked your parents before you went to the concert.
18. Pupils always .... listen to their teachers.
19. We .... go home now. Mum is waiting with dinner.
20. The rich in Europa and America .... do more for the poor in Africa.
21. You .... never provoke an angry teacher! You can only lose.
22. .... me to pick you up tomorrow morning?
23. At your age you .... know what is allowed and what is not.
24. ....n't you be at school, young man? What are you doing here?
25. Who .... do the dishes today? – Peter, I think.
26. Kenny, you know you .... call your father today.
27. You .... be very careful when you ride your bike into town.
28. ... . the boys to clean up after the party? – Yes, of course!
29. You really .... behave better when we have guests!
30. You .... be nicer to older people. They have deserved it.
31. Nobody .... know that we are here.
32. We ....n't leave Lisa alone now. She is very depressed.

(H) "ZUFÄLLIG"

- ***by chance (by accident)*** ▶ **durch Zufall, ohne Absicht oder Planung**

Columbus discovered America ***by chance / by accident*** *when he tried to reach India.*
Kolumbus entdeckte Amerika durch Zufall, als er versuchte, nach Indien zu gelangen.

We met the Millers ***by chance*** *while we were on holiday in the Bahamas.*
Wir trafen die Millers durch Zufall, als wir auf den Bahamas Urlaub machten.

Did you find this place ***by chance*** *or had you been looking for it?*
Haben Sie diesen Ort durch Zufall gefunden oder haben Sie danach gesucht?

- ***[happen] + infinitive*** ▶ **es geschah zufällig, es "passierte"**

Yesterday I ***happened to see*** *Alex and Sabrina in town.*
Gestern traf ich Alex und Sabrina zufällig in der Stadt.

If you ***happen to speak*** *with Joe, tell him I'm waiting for his call.*
Wenn du zufällig mit Joe sprichst, sag ihm, dass ich auf seinen Anruf warte.

Don't say such things about Danny! I ***happen to like*** *him.*
Sag nicht solche Sachen über Danny! Zufällig mag ich ihn.

68 Translate these sentences into good German.
Übersetze diese Sätze in gutes Deutsch.

1. I found your telephone number by chance as I was looking through my briefcase.
2. We happened to meet our neighbours at the supermarket.
3. I happened to hear that Joe is in town again.
4. Who happens to know where Mary lives now?
5. If you happen to see Tom, tell him to send me an email.
6. Marie Curie discovered radioactivity by accident.
7. We found out about the concert by chance.
8. Marcia saw the accident when she happened to look out of her window.
9. I happen to know about Charlie's adventure because I talked to his parents last week.
10. Mum found my black sweater by chance while she was looking for her jogging suit.
11. They found the thermal water by accident while they were digging for oil.
12. I won because I happened to know the correct answer.
13. If you happen to see a funny T-shirt, you can buy it.
14. Dad learned about the Porsche by chance when he was talking to a friend.
15. You don't happen to know where I've put my sun glasses, Mum?
16. If Joe happens to call again, you can ask him about his holidays in Alaska.
17. Theo bought these books by chance. He actually wanted to buy some CDs.
18. When we were in London last May, we happened to see the Queen's birthday parade.
19. J. K. Rowling became a writer by chance because she could not find a job.
20. If you should happen to win the lottery, what would you do?
21. Do you happen to know how many people were at the concert?
22. It was an interesting evening; nothing was planned, everything happened by chance.

69 Translate these sentences into good English.

Übersetze diese Sätze in gutes Englisch.

1. Durch Zufall hörten wir, dass das Haus zu kaufen war.
2. Du weißt nicht zufällig, wann die Nachrichten beginnen?
3. Gehen wir ins Kino! Heute habe ich zufällig Zeit.
4. Kennt jemand zufällig die Kombination für dieses Schloss?
5. Ich war zufällig im Garten, als du anriefst.
6. Berthold Schwarz entdeckte durch Zufall, wie man Schießpulver macht.
7. Mutter kaufte diese CD zufällig. Sie wollte eigentlich eine andere kaufen.
8. Wenn du zufällig mit Erica sprichst, wünsche ihr alles Gute zum Geburtstag.
9. Die Polizei fand die gestohlenen Juwelen durch Zufall während einer Verkehrskontrolle.
10. Ich bemerkte zufällig, wie ein Mann den USB-Stick entfernte. (to remove)
11. Wir sind nur durch Zufall hier; wir wollten eigentlich ins Kino gehen.
12. Ich fand den Einkaufszettel, als ich zufällig unter den Tisch schaute.
13. Wer erinnert sich zufällig an Emily's Telefonnummer?
14. Mach dir keine Sorgen! Ich weiß zufällig, wo der Ausgang ist.
15. Wenn jemand zufällig einen blauen Pullover findet, sagt es mir bitte.
16. Du magst Jazz nicht? Nun, zufällig bin ich ein Jazzfan!
17. Letztes Jahr gewann unsere Mannschaft zufällig das Finale, aber heuer werden sie verlieren.
18. Zufällig schien die Sonne, als wir aus dem Haus gingen.
19. Ich habe diesen Wein zufällig genommen. Ich hoffe, er schmeckt euch.
20. Dinge geschehen selten durch Zufall. Meist steckt ein Plan dahinter.
21. Durch Zufall kam Joe mit dem früheren Zug, so dass wir sofort beginnen konnten.
22. Zufällig fiel mir ein, wo Linda wohnte, aber sie war nicht zuhause.
23. Max erwähnte zufällig, dass er einen Arbeitsplatz gefunden hat.
24. Auf dem Nachhauseweg regnete es stark, aber zufällig hatte ich einen Regenschirm dabei.
25. Teresa und Maggie trafen sich nach fünf Jahren zufällig wieder.
26. Solltest du durch Zufall nach Washington kommen, musst du das Smithsonian Museum besuchen.
27. Hast du zufällig ein Fernglas mit? Ich möchte mir den Mond anschauen.
28. Ich habe diese Fotos zufällig gefunden. Gehören sie dir?
29. Hiram Bingham stieß 1911 durch Zufall auf eine große Ruinenstadt in den Anden von Peru.
30. Wir standen zufällig vor der Schule, als Enzo auf seinem neuen Mountainbike daherkam.
31. Zufällig sprach ich gestern mit Maria über dich.
32. Hast du gestern zufällig „Universum" gesehen?
33. Ein Farmarbeiter fand 1848 durch Zufall Gold im Sacramento River.
34. Zufällig weiß ich alles über diese Geschichte.
35. Ich traf Helen zufällig, als ich mit dem Hund spazieren ging.
36. Richard war zufällig zuhause, als ich anrief.
37. Natürlich kenne ich Mike. Zufällig ist er mein bester Freund!
38. Newton begann über die Schwerkraft nachzudenken, als ihm ein Apfel zufällig auf den Kopf fiel.
39. Durch Zufall machte ein Tourist ein Video von dem Flugzeugabsturz.
40. Sprich nicht so über Gina! Zufällig mag ich sie sehr!
41. Durch Zufall fand ich Vaters Autoschlüssel, als ich den Kühlschrank öffnete.

TENSES – Zeitstufen

70 Put the verbs into the correct tense and form.

Setze die Verben in die richtige Zeitstufe und Form.

1. During the school year I (go) .... to bed at ten every evening.
2. When I (be) .... in Athens with my family last summer, Dad (take) .... us to all the famous sights.
3. I (not see) .... Gina for over a week. I hope she is alright.
4. Mum and Dad (live) .... here for twenty years.
5. Listen to Joe! He (talk) .... about his childhood adventures again.
6. I (turn) .... off the computer after all the guests (leave) ....
7. I (cannot) .... close an eye last night because our neighbours (dance) .... and (sing) .... until two in the morning.
8. I'm sure they (ask) .... us lots of unpleasant questions tomorrow.
9. Joe (answer) .... your emails if he had read them in time.
10. Sue (be) .... sorry because she (hurt) .... me.
11. Mum (want) .... to visit her old teacher last Saturday, but she (not be) .... at home. She (try) .... it again soon.
12. Who (feed) .... the cats today? – I have, but they weren't really hungry.
13. This man (stand) .... over there since this morning. Who is he?
14. Can you hear the dogs? They (howl) .... like mad. Must be the moon!
15. At the end of this week, there (not be) .... any empty rooms in the hotel.
16. If you take this medicine, the pain (go) .... away very quickly.
17. Most birds (not sing) .... during the night, but the nightingale (do) ....
18. When I (wake) .... up this morning, the sun (shine) .... brightly and the birds (sing) .... in the trees.
19. I (read) .... "Hamlet" before I (see) .... it on TV.
20. One day you (be) .... sorry for what you (do) ....
21. We (get) .... a new headmistress at the beginning of this year. She (be) .... here for six months now, and she is okay.
22. (you, ever, try) .... "black" spaghetti? They taste strange, but good.
23. Mum (cook and bake) .... since this morning.
24. Be quiet, David! The President (speak) .... on TV and I want to listen.

25. Mum (cook) .... much better than I.

26. We will be lucky if nobody (find) .... us here.

27. The woman (die) .... before the doctor (arrive) ....

28. I (read) .... in bed last night when Mum (come) ....
in and (switch) .... off the light.

29. I promise I (never, use) .... your computer again!

30. My cousin (fly) .... in from the USA last Friday, but he (cannot) ....
.... stay long. He (leave) .... yesterday.

31. The young man promised the girl, "I (always, love) .... you!"

32. (you, ever, meet) .... Marcel Hirscher? – No, of course not.
But I (see) .... him on TV many times.

33. When Mr. Snyder (correct) .... our essays, he usually (use) ....
red ink.

34. What (you, do) ...., Mum? – I (make) ....
pizza for everybody. Can't you see? – Mmhhh! I (like) .... pizza!

35. We (talk) .... about tenses for three months now. That's too much for me!

36. If I (meet) .... you sooner, we could have gone to the dance together.

37. Dad (watch) .... TV while Jim and I (play) .... with
our game boy. We (do) .... this almost every evening.

38. (you, dance) .... with Sally last night? – No, I (do not) ....
.... I (not go) .... to the party.

39. Dad (study) .... law after he (leave) .... school.

40. Don't worry! Grandma (get) .... better soon.

41. Dad (smoke) .... a lot, but he (not smoke) ....
in the house. Mum (ask) .... him not to do so.

42. Mum, I think I (make) .... a silly mistake. Can you forgive me?

43. Dad says we (not go) .... skiing next year because it's so expensive.

44. The wind (blow) .... and the leaves (fall) ....
to the ground; it is autumn again! It (be) .... my favourite season!

45. Go to bed, Maggie! You (watch) .... those silly cartoons for hours!

46. You (get) .... better marks if you worked harder.

47. I (take) .... a bath when the telephone (ring) ....

48. I hope everybody (like) .... the cake. – Don't worry, I'm sure they will!

49. After we (sit) .... down, the film (start) ....

50. Mum (say) .... she (be) .... a naughty girl when she (be) .... as old as I (be) .... now, but I (not believe) .... her!
51. Mum (wear) .... gloves when she (drive) ....
52. Joe (take) .... all these photos himself. He is very talented.
53. If I had not run so fast, I (not win) .... the race.
54. What (you, do) .... , Melanie? – I (study) .... for the Maths test. (you, start) .... already? – No, I haven't.
55. My sister and I (learn) .... Spanish for two years, and we still like it.
56. We (just, go) .... to bed when I (see) .... a light in the garden. It (be) .... Mr. Somersby, our neighbour. He (look) .... for his cat "Minna".
57. "(you, marry) .... me?" Bill asked Monica.
58. World War II (begin) .... in 1938 and it (be) .... over in 1945. This means it (last) .... for six years.
59. If you don't inform the police, they (cannot) .... help you.
60. Grandpa (not drive) .... his car since his heart attack a year ago. Now he (want) .... to sell it.
61. You (not forget) .... me, will you?
62. These days my dad (not play) .... the guitar as often as he would like to.
63. If Sandra (know) .... about you and Joe, she would be disappointed.
64. Dave, why (you, make) .... such a noise? – I'm sorry, but I (try) .... to put nails in the wall so that I can hang up some pictures.
65. This letter (lie) .... on your desk for a week. Why (you, not open) .... it yet? – Well, I know what it (say) .... !
66. My parents (get) .... married on May 14th. They (be) .... married for almost fifteen years now.
67. I (lend) .... you the money if I knew you better.
68. After Mum (sell) .... her car, she (be) .... sorry.
69. Mum (work) .... for the same boss for six years. She says he is okay.
70. When I (come) .... home late last night, the radio (play) ...., the lights (be) .... still on, the dogs (lie) .... on the couch, and my sister (sleep) .... soundly on the living room floor.

A

accommodation	Unterkunft
act out	aufführen, darstellen
ads	Werbung, Reklame
advice	Rat
airstrip	Landebahn
among	unter, dazwischen, inmitten
another	noch eines, ein weiteres
answerphone	Anrufbeantworter
ant	Ameise
anthem	Hymne
appointment	Termin, Verabredung
argue	streiten, diskutieren
artist	Künstler
at last	endlich
auction	Auktion, Versteigerung
audience	Publikum
avalanche	Lawine
award	(einen Preis) verleihen

B

bankrupt	bankrott, pleite
bar of chocolate	Riegel Schokolade
bat	Fledermaus
bat	schlagen (beim Baseball)
bleary	verschlafen, versoffen
bomb threat	Bombendrohung
briefcase	Aktenkoffer
brilliant	glänzend, hervorragend, ausgezeichnet
brush	Pinsel, Bürste
bunch of keys	Schlüsselbund

C

cancel	absagen
celebration	Feier
cellar	Keller
changes	Veränderungen
chase (after)	(nach-, hinterher)jagen
cheat	schwindeln, betrügen, "schummeln"
chestnut tree	Kastanienbaum
circle	kreisen; Kreis
classmates	Mitschüler
coal mine	Kohlebergwerk
combat	Zweikampf
comfortable	bequem
company	Firma; Gesellschaft
compass	Zirkel
competition	Bewerb, Wettbewerb
conditions	Bedingungen
consequences	Folgen
(a) couple of	ein paar, einige
creature	Geschöpf, Wesen, Kreatur
cross oneself	sich bekreuzigen
crude oil	Rohöl
cutlery	Essbesteck

D

decent	anständig
declare the meeting over	die Sitzung für beendet erklären
defeat	besiegen
delighted	entzückt
depart	abfahren, abreisen
deserve	verdienen (Lob, Strafe)
destination	Ziel
destroy	zerstören
dial	wählen (Telefon)
diarrhea	Durchfall
disagree	anderer Meinung sein, nicht zustimmen
disappointed	enttäuscht
disguise	sich verkleiden
dishwasher	Geschirrspüler
drain pipe	Regenrohr
drawer	Schublade
drawing board	Zeichenbrett, -unterlage
dress up	sich verkleiden
drop (of oil)	(Öl-)Tropfen
drown	ertrinken
dustbin	Mistkorb
dwarf (dwarves)	Zwerg(e)
dye	färben (Haare)

E

economical	wirtschaftlich, sparsam
elect	wählen
electric drill	elektrische Bohrmaschine
embarrassed	verlegen, peinlich berührt
empty	münden (Fluss), entleeren (Gefäß)
engagement	Verlobung
entrance	Eingang
environment	Umwelt, Umgebung
escape	entkommen, flüchten, auskommen
event	Ereignis
explanation	Erklärung

F

faint	ohnmächtig werden
fairy tale	Märchen
fence	Zaun
fine	Geldstrafe
(be) fined	zu einer Geldstrafe verurteilt werden

fine print	das Kleingedruckte
fire extinguisher	Feuerlöscher
flat	Wohnung, Appartement
fleet	Flotte
flight	Flug, Flucht
flight attendant	Flugbegleiter(in)
flood	überfluten, überschwemmen
fool around	herumalbern
foreign	fremd, ausländisch
former	früher, ehemalig
founding members	Gründungsmitglieder
fun park	Vergnügungspark
fur coat	Pelzmantel
furniture	Möbel

G

gain (three kilos)	zunehmen (Gewicht)
garage	Garage, Werkstätte
gather	sammeln
generous	großzügig
go (well) together	(gut) zusammenpassen
grasshopper	Heuschrecke
graze	grasen, weiden

H

habit	Brauch, Angewohnheit
handsome	gut aussehend, fesch
headmaster	(Schul-)Direktor
headmistress	(Schul-)Direktorin
hedgehog	Igel
hiking	Wandern
Hispanics	Spanisch-Sprechende in den USA
honeymoon	Flitterwochen
honoured	geehrt
howl	heulen
humble	bescheiden

I

icicle	Eiszapfen
immediately	sofort
impress	beeindrucken
improve	verbessern
incident	Vorfall
indeed	in der Tat, wirklich
insulate	isolieren, abdichten
invisible	unsichtbar

J

jack	Wagenheber
jail	Gefängnis

L

landing strip	Landestreifen
last, -ed	dauern
lawyer	Anwalt
lecture	Vortrag
lenient	milde, tolerant, nicht streng
locker	Spind
locker room	(Spieler-)Garderobe
look alike	gleich aussehen
lose (three kilos)	abnehmen (Gewicht)

M

madman	Verrückter
make an appointment	einen Termin ausmachen
make up one's mind	beschließen, sich entscheiden
mammal	Säugetier
manual	Handbuch
mean	gemein, mies
message	Botschaft, Nachricht
miracle	Wunder
mood	Stimmung
mostly	hauptsächlich
mountainside	(Berg-)Hang
mugger	Räuber (auf der Straße)
mushrooms	Pilze

N

name tag	Namensschild
nap (take a ...)	Schläfchen (machen)
nearby	nahe, in der Nähe
nightingale	Nachtigall
notice	bemerken
nurse	stillen

O

ordinary	gewöhnlich

P

pain	Schmerz(en)
passer-by	Passant, ein Vorübergehender
peel	schälen, Schale
perform	aufführen, spielen, darstellen
performance	Aufführung
permission	Erlaubnis
pick (someone) up	(jemand) abholen
pickpocket	Taschendieb
plaster cast	Gipsverband
platypus	Schnabeltier
pleasure	Vergnügen
pollution	(Umwelt-)Verschmutzung
prefer	bevorzugen, vorziehen

present	überreichen
pretend	so tun als ob, vortäuschen
prevent	verhindern, vermeiden
prison	Gefängnis
pronounce	aussprechen
protect	schützen, beschützen
provoke	provozieren, herausfordern
punch	schlagen
puncture	Loch im Reifen, Panne
punish	bestrafen

R

rafter	Balken
rain cats and dogs	in Strömen regnen, schütten
rash	(Haut-)Ausschlag
receive	erhalten, empfangen
redecorate	umgestalten
refugee	Flüchtling
remarkable	bemerkenswert, beachtlich
remove	entfernen
report to	sich melden bei
resort	Urlaubsort, Kurort
rise	entspringen (Fluss)
rubbish	Müll, Mist
rule, -ed	regieren, beherrschen

S

satisfied	zufrieden
schedule	Zeitplan, Stundenplan
sculptor	Bildhauer
see the doctor	zum Arzt gehen
sensible	vernünftig
serious(ly)	ernst, ernsthaft
several	mehrere
sewers	Kanalisation, Abwasserkanäle
shape	Figur, Kondition
share	teilen
shovel	Schaufel
show around	herumführen
sick	übel, krank
skilfull	geschickt
skills	Fähigkeiten
slope	Hang
slug	Nacktschnecke
snore	schnarchen
solve a problem	ein Problem lösen
sound(ly)	fest
spectators	Zuschauer
spell	buchstabieren
squirrel	Eichhörnchen
steam engine	Dampfmaschine
stock report	Börsenbericht
straw hat	Strohhut
stuffy (air)	stickig (Luft)
stumble	stolpern
success	Erfolg
suntan	Sonnenbräune
superb(ly)	herrlich, prächtig
supply	versorgen
surface	Oberfläche
survive	überleben
swallow	Schwalbe
swear	schwören

T

tear gas	Tränengas
telescope	Fernrohr
threat	Drohung, Bedrohung
tomb [tu:m]	Grabmal, Grabstätte
trombone	Posaune
trust	vertrauen
tune	Melodie

U

uncertain	unsicher, ungewiss
underwear	Unterwäsche
uneasy	unbehaglich, unwohl
unhurt	unverletzt
unpleasant	unangenehm
unsafe	unsicher, gefährlich

V

valley floor	Talboden
votes	Stimmen (bei einer Wahl)

W

wardrobe	Kleiderschrank
waste	Verschwendung, Vergeudung
weeping willow	Trauerweide ("weinende Weide")
well	Brunnen, Quelle
whipped cream	Schlagobers
whistle	pfeifen
wind up (watch)	aufziehen (Uhr)
wipe out	auslöschen, vernichten
witness	Zeuge

Y

youth hostel	Jugendherberge

A

abgeben (Arbeit)	hand in
abheben (Flugzeug)	take off
ablösen, auswechseln	change
absagen	cancel
abschreiben	copy
absperren, zusperren	lock
Aktentasche, -koffer	briefcase
annehmen	accept, take on
Anzug	suit
atmen	breathe
aufpassen	look after
Aufsatz	essay
auftragen (Makeup)	put on
(sich etwas) ausborgen	borrow
(Formular) ausfüllen	fill in (a form)
Ausrede	excuse
Ausstellung	exposition, exhibition
austauschen	exchange
auswechseln, ablösen	change

B

begleiten	come with (her), accompany
beitreten	join
(sich) beklagen	complain
beruhigen	calm down
beschützen	protect
bestehen (Prüfung)	pass
(nicht) bestehen	fail
Busausweis	bus pass

D

Drogenhändler	drug dealer
durchblättern	look through
durchfallen, nicht bestehen	fail

E

eigentlich	actually
einreisen	enter
einschlafen	fall asleep
einziehen (Haus)	move in(to)
entfernen	remove
enttäuschen	disappoint
erfahren	hear, learn
(sich) erholen	recover
erkennen	recognise
Erlaubnis	permission

F

färben (Haare)	dye
Feier	celebration
Fernglas	binoculars
fernhalten	keep away
Flugzeugabsturz	plane crash
Formular	form
Fremder	stranger

G

geehrt	honoured
gegenüber	opposite
gehorchen	obey
Gesetz (beschließen)	(pass) law
gießen (Blumen)	water
graben	dig

H

Haarschnitt	haircut
Hymne	anthem

I

(sich) irren	be wrong

J

jagen	hunt – hunted – hunted
jammern	complain
je, jemals	ever

K

kennen lernen	meet; get to know
krabbeln	crawl

L

lackieren	paint
leiden	suffer
leihen	lend
(sich) lustig machen über	make fun of

M

marschieren	march
Möbelkatalog	furniture catalogue
Moschee	mosque

N

nachahmen	imitate, copy
nachsitzen lassen	give detention
Narbe	scar
nicht bestehen (Prüfung)	fail
Not	misery

P

pflanzen	plant
plaudern	talk
posieren	pose
Prüfung	exam, test
pünktlich	on time

R

raten (Rat geben)	advise
raten (vermuten)	guess
Rathaus	city hall, town hall
Rätsel lösen	solve the puzzle
Rechnung	bill
Rede	speech
reichen	pass

S

Saurier	dinosaur
schenken	give
Schiedsrichter	referee
Schießpulver	gunpowder
schlagen (Baseball)	bat
Schlittschuh laufen	skate
Schloss (zum absperren)	lock
schnarchen	snore
Schweinefleisch	pork
Schwerkraft	gravity
sich beklagen	complain
sich erholen	recover
sich irren	be wrong
sich lustig machen über	make fun of
spannend	thrilling, exciting
spazieren	walk
spielen (um Geld)	gamble
Stirn	forehead
stören	disturb
Streifen	stripe(s)
streiten	argue, fight, quarrel
stürzen	fall

T

Tat	action
toll	great
Truthahn	turkey

U

überprüfen	check
überzeugen	convince
um Geld spielen	gamble
unhöflich	impolite
unmöglich	impossible

V

verletzen	hurt
verschieben (zeitlich)	postpone
versinken	sink
verständigen	inform, notify
verwenden	use
vorbeiten	prepare
Vorfall	incident

W

wegziehen	move away
wehen (Wind)	blow
weinen	cry
werden	get, be, become
Wettbewerb	competition
Wiese	meadow
Wunder	miracle

Z

zählen	count
Zelt	tent
zufrieden	satisfied, content
zurückreden	talk back
zusperren, absperren	lock
zweifeln	doubt [daut]

base form (infinitive)	past form (past tense)	3rd form (past participle)	Deutsch
to be	was/were	been	sein
to beat	beat	beaten	schlagen
to become	became	become	werden
to begin	began	begun	beginnen
to bite	bit	bitten	beißen
to blow	blew	blown	blasen, wehen
to break	broke	broken	brechen
to bring	brought	brought	bringen
to build	built	built	bauen
to burn	burnt	burnt	brennen
to buy	bought	bought	kaufen
to catch	caught	caught	fangen
to choose	chose	chosen	wählen
to come	came	come	kommen
to cost	cost	cost	kosten
to cut	cut	cut	schneiden
to dig	dug	dug	graben
to do	did	done	tun, machen
to draw	drew	drawn	zeichnen, ziehen
to drink	drank	drunk	trinken
to drive	drove	driven	fahren (selbst)
to eat	ate	eaten	essen
to fall	fell	fallen	fallen
to feel	felt	felt	fühlen
to fight	fought	fought	kämpfen
to find	found	found	finden
to fly	flew	flown	fliegen
to forbid	forbade	forbidden	verbieten
to forget	forgot	forgotten	vergessen
to freeze	froze	frozen	frieren
to get	got	got	bekommen
to give	gave	given	geben
to go	went	gone	gehen
to grow	grew	grown	wachsen
to hang	hung	hung	hängen
to have	had	had	haben
to hear	heard	heard	hören
to hide	hid	hidden	verstecken
to hit	hit	hit	schlagen
to hold	held	held	halten
to hurt	hurt	hurt	verletzen
to keep	kept	kept	behalten, halten
to know	knew	known	kennen, wissen

base form (infinitive)	past form (past tense)	3rd form (past participle)	Deutsch
to leave	left	left	verlassen
to lend	lent	lent	leihen
to let	let	let	lassen
to lie	lay	lain	liegen
to lose	lost	lost	verlieren
to make	made	made	machen
to mean	meant	meant	bedeuten
to meet	met	met	treffen
to pay	paid	paid	bezahlen
to put	put	put	legen, setzen
to read	read	read	lesen
to ride	rode	ridden	fahren, reiten
to ring	rang	rung	läuten
to rise	rose	risen	sich erheben
to run	ran	run	laufen, rennen
to say	said	said	sagen
to see	saw	seen	sehen
to sell	sold	sold	verkaufen
to send	sent	sent	schicken
to shake	shook	shaken	schütteln
to steal	stole	stolen	stehlen
to shine	shone	shone	scheinen
to shoot	shot	shot	schießen
to show	showed	shown	zeigen
to shut	shut	shut	schließen
to sing	sang	sung	singen
to sit	sat	sat	sitzen
to sleep	slept	slept	schlafen
to speak	spoke	spoken	sprechen
to spend	spent	spent	verbrauchen
to take	took	taken	nehmen
to teach	taught	taught	lehren
to tear	tore	torn	(zer)reißen
to tell	told	told	erzählen (+ object)
to think	thought	thought	denken, glauben
to throw	threw	thrown	werfen
to wake	woke	woken	aufwachen, wecken
to wear	wore	worn	tragen (Kleidung)
to weep	wept	wept	weinen
to win	won	won	gewinnen
to write	wrote	written	schreiben

ISBN 978-3-7058-9265-1

ISBN 978-3-7058-9263-7

ISBN 978-3-7058-9264-4